Ksatriya Clans in Buddhist India

Ksatriya Clans in Buddhist India

BIMALA CHARAN LAW, M. A., B. L.

GYAN

Published by

Gyan Publishing House
5, Ansari Road
Daryaganj, New Delhi-110002
Phone: 011-47034999, 9811692060
E-mail: books@gyanbooks.com

Distribution Network
gyanbooks.com
India, USA, Canada, UK, Australia, France

ISBN: 978-81-212-8736-4 (PB)
First Published, 1922

2nd Impression 2023

Printed at: Gyan Press, Delhi.

Ksatriya Clans in Buddhist India
Author: Bimala Charan Law

KSATRIYA CLANS
IN
BUDDHIST INDIA

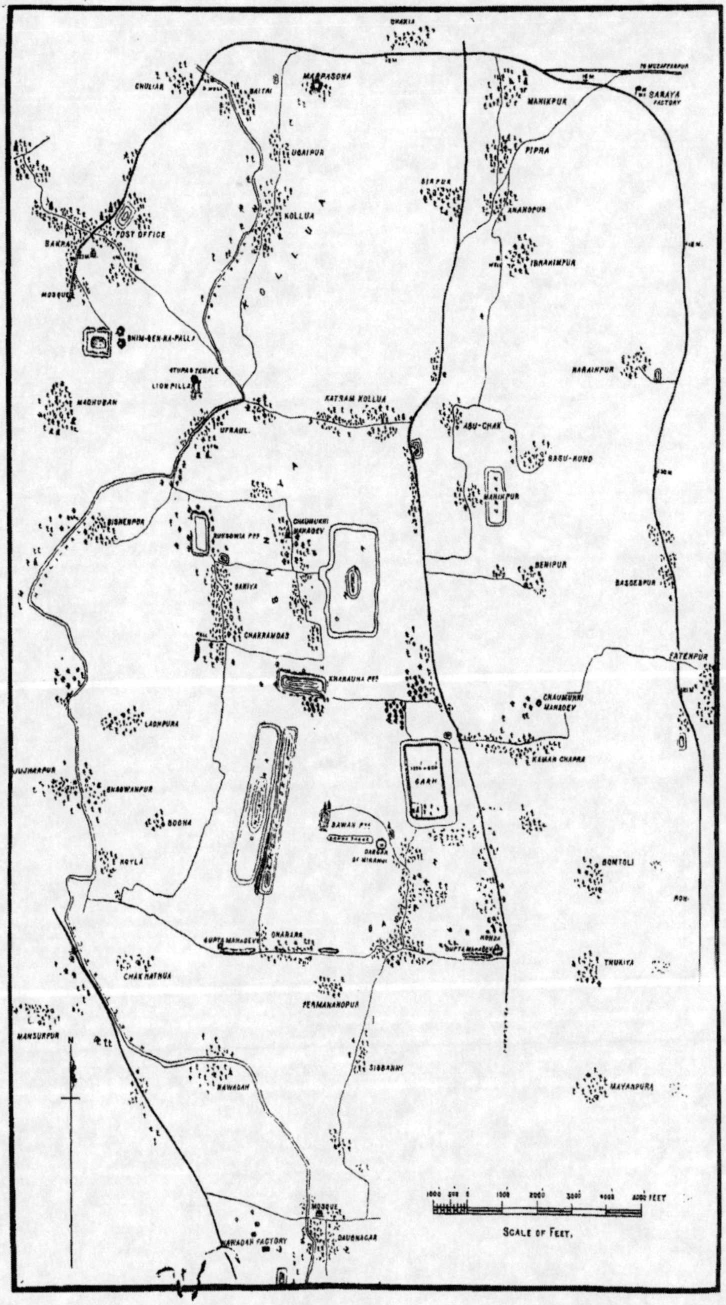

Map of Vaisālī, the Capital of the Licchavis.

Ksatriya Clans in Buddhist India

BY

BIMALA CHARAN LAW, M.A., B.L.
FELLOW, ROYAL HISTORICAL SOCIETY, LONDON.

WITH A FOREWORD BY

THE HON'BLE SIR ASUTOSH MOOKERJEE, KT.,
C. S. I.
VICE-CHANCELLOR, UNIVERSITY OF CALCUTTA.

Calcutta and Simla
THACKER SPINK & Co
1922.

TO

MY GRANDFATHER

THE LATE BABU JAYGOBIND LAW, C.I.E.

THIS VOLUME

IS

WITH GREAT RESPECT AND REVERENCE

DEDICATED.

FOREWORD

I have read with great interest the monograph on Kṣatriya clans in Buddhist India prepared by Mr. Bimala Charan Law, a distinguished graduate of our University, who has already given promise of solid work as a research student. The work is divided into two parts; the first deals with the Licchavis, the second is devoted to the Videhas, the Mallas, the Śākyas and the minor clans. As is well-known, there is no systematic account in the early Pāli books of the political conditions of Northern India during the life-time of the Buddha. A picture of society in Buddhistic times can consequently be visualised, only after a systematic account has been drawn up from scattered references in a vast historical, philosophical and socio-religious literature. From this point of view, the undertaking of Mr. Law is of special importance. He has not contented himself with an outline of the political history of those times, but has treated as well of manners and customs, of religion and philosophy, and of the judicial and administrative machinery. Mr. Law does not profess to have investigated the history of all the republics actually mentioned by name in the oldest Pāli records as also those discoverable from the writings of the Greeks who visited India; many of those tribes, as we know, have not yet been identified, but a fairly accurate idea may be formed of their activities, their judicial and administrative functions. We trust Mr. Law will continue his investigations and ultimately give us a complete history of all the Kṣatriya clans which flourished in Buddhistic and post-Buddhistic times.

The 8th August, 1922. ASUTOSH MOOKERJEE.

PREFACE

The present treatise attempts a connected history of some of the Kṣatriya clans in ancient India in the time of the Buddha, viz., the Licchavis, the Videhas, the Mallas, the Śākyas, and some minor clans. This part of the history of India has up to now received very scant attention from historians. Dr. Rhys Davids in his Buddhist India simply mentions these clans. The Hinayāna Buddhist literature contains a good many references to the important clans under review, while the Mahāyāna Buddhist literature is very poor in this respect. So far as the minor clans are concerned, the nothern Buddhist literature is silent, while the southern Buddhist literature records a very meagre account of them. Sanskrit literature is of no great help to us. I have consulted the Tibetan literature as well as the works of English, French and German authors. In translating the texts, I have tried to be as much literal as possible, and I have retained the translators' language in making use of the English translations.

Recently I wrote a paper on the Licchavis in ancient India which has been published in the Journal of the Asiatic Society of Bengal (New Series. Vol. XVII. 1921. No. 3) where I tried to give a brief history of them. I am indebted to

Mahāmahopādhyāya Hara Prasād Śāstrī, C. I. E., M. A. and Dr. D. R. Bhāndārkar, M. A., Ph. D. whose sound advice and valuable suggestions I readily availed of while the paper was passing through the press. I am indebted to many of my friends and teachers among whom may be mentioned Dr. B. M. Barua, M. A., D. Litt. (London), Mr. Haran Chandra Chakladar, M. A., Mr. Bepin Vehary Gupta, M. A., Mr. Surendra Nath Muzumder Sastri, M. A., P. R. S., Mr. Nandalal Dey, M. A., B. L., Mr. Benode Lall Mukherjee, M. A., B. L., Mr. Hari Pada Ghosh, B. A., Pandit Kālipada Tarkācārya, Kāvya-vyākaraṇatarkatīrtha, Pandit Dakṣinā Charan Bhattācārya, Mr. Balai Chand Dutt, B. A., and Mr. Balai Lall Dutt, B. A.

For the map and the photographs and for kind permission to reproduce them in this book, my thanks are due to Sir John Marshall Kt., K.C.I.E. Director-General of Archæology, India and Lionel Heath Esq., Curator, Central Museum, Lahore.

The Hon'ble Mr. Justice Ashutosh Mukherjee, Kt. C. S. I., M. A, D. L., D. Sc., Ph. D., F. R. A.S.F.R.S.E., F.A.S.B. Saraswatī, Sātravācaspati, Sambuddhāgamacakkavattī, has laid me under a deep debt of obligation by writing the foreword to this book.

24 Sukea's Street,
Calcutta.
6th June 1922.

Bimala Charan Law.

CONTENTS.

MAP AND ILLUSTRATIONS.

BIBLIOGRAPHY.

1. Adhyātma Rāmāyaṇa edited by Kāli Saṅkar Vidyāratṇa.
2. Aitareya Brāhmaṇa.
3. Anargharāghava.
4. Ancient Geography of India by Cunningham.
5. Aṅguttara Ṇikāya (P. T. S.)
6. Archæological Survey of India, Annual Report, 1903—04.
7. Archæological Survey Reports Vols I & XVI.
8. Arthaśāstra of Kauṭilya edited by Shāmaśāstry, 2nd Ed.
9. Arthaśāstra of Kauṭilya translated by Shāmaśāstry.
10. Aśoka—Vincent Smith, 2nd Edition.
11. Atharvasaṃhitā—Translated by Whitney and revised and edited by C. R. Lanman.
12. Atharvavedasaṃhitā—Roth & Whitney.
13. Avadānakalpalatā (Bibliotheca Indica Series)
14. Bhaviṣyapurāṇa.
15. Book of the Kindred Sayings, Part I.(P.T.S.)
16. Buddhism—Monier Williams.
17. Buddhist India by Dr. Rhys Davids.
18. Buddhist Records of the Western World. (Si-yu-ki)
19. Buddhist Suttas (S. B. E.) Vol. XI.
20. Carmichael Lectures—1918.

21. Chārudatta.
22. Corpus Inscriptionum Indicarum—Fleet.
23. Dhammapadam (old edition)—Fausboll.
24. Dialogues of the Buddha, (Sacred Books of the Buddhists)—T. W. & C. A. F. Rhys Davids.
25. Dīgha-Nikāya (P. T. S.)
26. Divyāvadāna, Edited by Cowell & Neil.
27. Early History of India (3rd Edition)—V. A. Smith.
28. Fick's Social Organisation in North-East India in Buddha's time translated by Dr. S. K. Maitra.
29. Gaina Sūtras (S. B. E.) translated by Jacobi.
30. Geschichte der Indischen Litteratur—Dr. M. Winternitz.
31. Gupta coins—Allen.
32. Indian Antiquary.
33. Indian coins—Rapson.
34. Indische Studien edited by Weber.
35. Inscriptions of Aśoka Edited by D. R. Bhāndārkar and S. N. Majumdār.
36. Jātaka (Faüsboll)
37. Jātaka (Edited by Cowell)
38. Journal of the Asiatic Society of Bengal, Vols. XII, VI, LXIX.
39. Journal of the Department of Letters, Calcutta University, Vol. III.
40. Journals of the Royal Asiatic Society 1902, 1913.

41. Karmaśaṭaka translated from Tibetan by M. L. Feer.
42. Lalitavistara Edited by E. Lefmann.
43. Laws of Manu (S. B. E.)
44. Le Mahāvastu Edited by E. Senart.
45. Life of the Buddha by Rockhill.
46. Life of Hiuen Tsiang—Beal.
47. Mahābhārata (Vangavāsī Edition)
48. Mahāvagga—atthakathā (Ceylonese Edition)
49. Mahāvaṃsa—translated by Geiger.
50. Mahāvaṃsa Ṭīkā (Ceylonese Edition)
51. Majjhima Nikāya (P. T. S.)
52. Mānavadharmaśāstra Edited by Jolly.
53. Manual of Buddhism by Spence Hardy.
54. Manual of Indian Buddhism by Kern.
55. Mṛcchakoṭika Edited by Jīvānanda Vidyāsāgara.
56. Mudrārākṣasa Edited by Aswini Kumar Vidyābhūṣaṇ.
57. Origin of the Bengali Script by Mr. R. D. Banerjee.
58. Paramatthadīpanī (P. T. S.)
59. Paramatthajotikā on the Khuddakapāṭha (P. T. S.)
60. Petavatthu (P. T. S.)
61. Petavatthu-aṭṭhakathā (Ceylonese Edition)
62. Prācīn Mudrā by Babu Rakhaldas Banerjee.
63. Psalms of the Brethren—Mrs. Rhys Davids.
64. Psalms of the Sisters—Mrs. Rhys Davids.
65. Public Administration in Ancient India by Dr. P. Banerjee.

66. Rāmāyaṇa (Bombay Edition)
67. Romantic Legend of the Śākya Buddha by Beal.
68. Sacred Books of the East, Vols IX, XVII, XIX, XLIX.
69. Saṃyutta Nikāya (P. T. S.)
70. Satapatha Brāhmaṇa (S. B. E.)
71. Sumaṅgalavilāsinī (Burmese Edition)
72. Sumaṅgalavilāsinī (P. T. S.)
73. Tārānāth's Geschichte des Buddhismus in India translated into German by Anton Schiefner.
74. Travels of Fā-Hien—Beal.
75. Travels of Fā-Hien—Legge.
76. Travels of Fā-Hien & Sung yun—S. Beal.
77. T. Watters, On Yuan Chwang Edited by Dr. T. W. Rhys Davids & Bushell.
78. Uvāsagadasāo (Bibliotheca Indica Series)
79. Vaijayantī Edited by Oppert.
80. Vaiṣṇavism, Śaivaism and minor religious systems by Sir. R. G. Bhāndārkar.
81. Vāṅglār Itihāsa by Mr. R. D. Banerjee.
82. Vedic Index by Macdonell & Keith.
83. Vinaya Piṭaka Edited by Oldenberg.
84. Vinaya Texts (S. B. E.)
85. Viṣṇupurāṇa (Vaṅgavāsī Edition)
86. Vrihadāraṇyka Upaniṣad (Ânandāśraṃ Edition)
87. Vrihat Viṣṇupurāṇa.

Ksatriya Clans in Buddhist India.

PART I.

THE LICCHAVIS.

CHAPTER I.

Name and Origin.

Introductory

The Licchavis were a great and powerful people in Eastern India in the sixth century before Christ. Their peculiar form of government, their democratic institutions, their manners and customs, their religion and philosophy, afford us glimpses of India of the transition period, when the ancient Vedic culture was making a fresh development and undergoing a novel transformation under the influence of that speculative activity out of which emerged the two great religions of Jainism and Buddhism. Fortunately for us, Buddhist literature, and to a less extent the Jaina sacred books, have preserved for us facts and comments which, though in bits and fragments, are yet sufficient to hold up before our eyes a living picture of this interesting people. From the account of their political institutions that can be gleaned from the Pāli Buddhist

Canon, we get an insight into the democratic ideas of statecraft and government that prevailed among the majority of the Aryan clans that peopled northern India before the imperialistic policy of the Mauryas grew and developed, as we have it on the authority of the great Brāhmin statesman whose policy and activity were responsible, in no little measure, for the foundation of the Maurya Empire. This great people who were one of the earliest and most devoted followers of Jainism and Buddhism, whose high character, unity, power of organisation, and religious devotion were held up by Śākyamuni himself as a model for the Buddhist congregation to follow, deserve to be studied with as much care and attention as the materials at our command will require or permit. Such a close study will, we think, well repay the trouble bestowed upon it and with this hope we proceed to piece together the bits and scraps that lie scattered in literature, and to a smaller extent, in epigraphs and coins.

The name

We find in Indian literature the name of this great people in slightly varying forms—Licchavi, Licchivi, Lecchavi, Lecchaī and so on. Throughout the Pāli Canon the name invariably occurs in the form "Licchavi." In some of the Buddhist Sanskrit texts, e. g., the Divyāvadāna,[1] the name

1. *Divyāvadāna* edited by E. B. Cowell and R. A. Neil. pp. 55-56, 136.

is found in the same form, i. e., "Licchavi," but in others, for example, the Mahāvastu Avadāna, the usual form is Lecchavi.[1] In the Chinese translations of the Buddhist sacred books, the name occurs in both the forms Licchavi and Lecchavi,[2] and this is what is expected, as these translations are based on the Sanskrit Buddhist texts. The Mahāvastu form, Lecchavi, answers very well to the Prākrit form, Lecchaī, as we find it in another set of works that claim to be contemporaneous in origin with the Buddhist Canon, namely, the Jaina sacred literature which, according to some scholars,[3] began to be composed by perhaps the direct disciples of Mahāvīra in the first century after his death, or at the latest, in the next century, by the time of Candragupta Maurya when the first council of the Jainas was held at Pāṭaliputra.[3]

In the Sūtrakritāñga, one of the earliest works of the Jaina sacred literature, we meet with the name Lecchaī [4] and the same form occurs in the Kalpasūtra attributed to Bhadravāhu who is considered to have been a contemporary of the great Maurya Emperor,

1. *Mahāvastu* edited by E. Senart, pp 1, 254 etc.

2. T. Watters—*On Yuan Chwang,* Vol. II, p. 77.

3. Dr. M. Winternitz, *Geschichte der Indischen Litteratur* II Band, p. 295.

4. *Kalpasūtra.* § 128. *Sirikalpasūtram,* Bhavnagar edition p. 192 See also *Jaina Sūtras* by H. Jacobi, S. B. E. vol. xxii, p. 266 and Vol. xlv, part. II, p. 321. f. n. 3.

Cāndragupta. The Jaina commentators equate the Prākrit Lecchaī with Sanskrit Lecchakī,[1] and according to the laws of phonetic transformation, the Sanskrit Lecchavi and Lecchakī would both lead to Lecchaī in Prākrit. In the form Lecchakī, however, the name does never occur in Sanskrit literature in which the earliest mention, so far as we have been able to ascertain, of this powerful people is in Kauṭilya's Arthaśāstra, where they are called Licchivis, and we read of them that "the corporations of Licchivika, Vṛjika, Mallaka, Madraka, Kukura, Kuru, Pāñcāla and others live by the title of a rājā."[2] We next find them mentioned in the Mānava Dharmaśāstra (X. 22). Here, of course, there are some *variæ lectiones*; the anonymous Kashmirian comment on the Mānava Dharmaśāstra reads *Lichavi* which approximates very closely to the Buddhistic form and Medhātithi and Govindarāja, the two earliest commentators of the Mānava Dharmaśāstra, read *Licchivi* and this reading tallies exactly with the name as given by Kauṭilya; this form, therefore, represents the earliest spelling of this word in the Brāhmanic Sanskrit literature. It is only Kulluka

1. *Jaina Sūtras* by H. Jacobi S. B. E., Vol. xxii, part I; p. 266. n.
2. Kauṭilya's Arthaśāstra translated by R. Shamśastry B. A. p. 455. The Sanskrit text has :—"Licchivika-Vṛjika-Mallaka-Madraka-Kukura-Kuru-Pāñcālādayo Rājaśabdopajivinah." The 'Ka' at the end of the words does not change the meaning at all.

Bhaṭṭa, the Bengali commentator, who reads *Nicchivi* in this verse of Manu ; Rāghavānanda, another commentator, follows Kulluka, as he does everywhere else, both in spelling as well as in interpretation, and the ordinary printed editions of the Manusamhitā that implicity follow Kulluka, have adopted this reading.[1] Both Jolly and Bühler, the two great authorities on Manu, have accepted the form *Licchivi* which is without doubt the correct reading. Kulluka who wrote apparently in the fifteenth century and was thus younger by about six hundred years than Medhātithi and by about three hundred years than Govindarāja, was evidently misled by the similarity of the letters 'N' and 'L' as they were written in Bengali in the fifteenth century, and as they are still found to be written even in modern Bengali manuscripts.

Already in the early years of the eleventh century, the Bengali forms of *Na* and *La* had developed almost completely from the eastern variety of the north Indian alphabet as we find from the Kṛṣṇa Dwārika temple inscription of the fifteenth year of Nayapāla ; but a little later on, towards the end of the century, we find in the Deopārā inscription of Vijaya Sena that "*La* has a peculiar form, resembling *La* which is still

1. For the various readings see *Mānava Dharmaśāstra* edited by J. Jolly Ph. D. p. 325. See also *The Laws of Manu* by G. Bühler, S. B. E. Vol. XXV. p. 406. notes.

found in some cases in modern Bengali manuscripts where *La* is denoted by a dot placed under *Na*."[1] Coming down still later, nearer the time of Kulluka, we observe that "the Kamauli grant shows the use of the peculiar twelfth century form of *la* which is also found in the Deopārā *Praśasti* and the Tetrawan image inscription of the second year of Rāmapāla. The form of this letter is the same as the *Ta* of the modern Nāgarī;"[2] and this peculiar *Ta*-shaped form also occurs in many other inscriptions of a later date, and Mr. R. D. Banerji from whom we have quoted above, observes, "the *Ta* shaped form of *la* still survives in Bengali where a dot is put under *na* to denote *la*."[3] This dot, however, was often omitted by scribes and it is no wonder, therefore, that Kulluka, or rather the scribes who copied his work, read and wrote *Nicchivi* in the place of Licchivi. Hence we have no hesitation in rejecting Kulluka's reading *Nicchivi* and any attempt to connect the Licchavis with *Nisibis* in Persia[4] on such a flimsy foundation is not worthy of much consideration. Kulluka in his reading has made the same mistake as is found in Nandanācārya's commentary called *Nandinī* or *Manvarthavyā-*

1. R. D. Banerji, *The Origin of the Bengali Script.* Cal. Univ. 1919, p. 82.
2. Ibid, p. 108.
3. Ibid, p. 109.
4. Mahāmahopādhyāya Dr. Satish Ch. Vidyābhūṣaṇ, *Indian Antiquary*, Vol. XXXVII, pp. 78-80.

khyāna where we have the name in the form *Lichikhi*,[1] ख being evidently a clerical error for च. It should be observed, however, that here also the word begins with *l* and not *n*. Nowhere but in Kulluka and the editions dependent on him do we meet with the form with an initial *N*.

Next, that Nicchivi was only an accidental clerical error and had nothing to do with the name of the people we are dealing with, appears from the Sanskrit inscriptions of the early Gupta Emperors. In the Allāhābād posthumous stone pillar inscription of Samudragupta, that great monarch is described as the *Licchavi-dauhitra* or 'the son of the daughter of the Licchavis,'[2] so that we have here the very same form as in the Pāli Buddhist works. We have the same form in many other inscriptions of the monarchs of this family, for example, in the Mathurā stone inscription of Candragupta II,[3] the Bilsād stone pillar inscription of Kumāra Gupta of the year 96,[4] the Behār stone pillar inscription of Skandagupta,[5] etc. On the other hand, the other variant, Licchivi, is found to occur in the Bhitāri stone pillar inscription of Skanda Gupta[6] and

1. Jolly, *Mānavadharmaśâstra*, p. 325.
2. *Inscriptions of the Early Gupta Kings*, edited by J. F. Fleet—*Corpus Inscriptionum Indicarum*, Vol. III, p. 8.
3. Fleet, op. cit p. 27.
4. Ibid., p. 43.
5. Ibid., p. 50.
6. Ibid., p. 53.

the Gayā copper plate inscription of Samudra Gupta,[1] which is considerd to be spurious. Some of the coins of Candragupta I have the name Licchavi on them. Moreover, in the inscription of the Nepāl kings who claim to have descended from the family of the Licchavis, the expression used is always Licchavi-kula-ketu, 'the banner or glory of the Licchavi family.'[2] In the Sanskrit inscriptions, therefore, the usual form of the name is Licchavi, and the form Licchivi is also met with occasionally. Coming now to the form of the name as used in countries outside India, we have seen that in the Chinese translations which are based on Sanskrit Buddhist texts, the form is Licchavi or Lecchavi ; Fā Hien speaks of them as Licchavis[3] ; in Hiuen Tsiang's *Records of the Western World*, the form is Li-ch'e p'o which would correspond to the form Licchavi.[4] The Tibetans who began to have the Buddhist books translated into their own language from the eighth century A. D, have also the form *Licchavi*. In the Tibetan Dulva from which Rockhill quotes in his *Life of the Buddha* (p. 97 foll.) the form is Licchavi. Schiefner, in his German translation of Tārānātha's *History of Buddhism*

1. Fleet, *Inscriptions of the Early Gupta Kings*, *Corpus Inscriptionum Indicarum* Vol. III, p. 256

2. Ibid. p. 175 ff. *Indian Antiquary*, Vol, IX, p. 168. ff.

3. Legge, Fa-Hien, pp. 71, 76.

4. *Buddhist Records of the Western World* by S. Beal, Vol. II. p. 73.

in India, spells the word as *Litschtschhavi*,[1] the consonantal group *tsch* representing, according to German orthography, the Indian च (c).

The Licchavis were neither Tibetan nor Iranian in their origin, but there is very clear evidence in the Buddhist literature to show that they belonged to the Aryan ruling caste—the Kṣatriya. In the Mahāparinibbāṇa Suttanta to which we have already referred, we read that after the decease of the Buddha, his body was preserved for a week by the Mallas of Kuśīnārā, while in the meantime, the news of the passing away of the Master reached the people of the countries far and near. Now the Licchavis of Vaiśālī claimed a share of the remnants of his body. We read here, "And the Licchavis of Veśālī heard the news that the Exalted One had died at Kuśīnārā. And the Licchavis of Veśālī sent a messenger to the Mallas, saying: "The Exalted One was a Kṣatriya and so are we. We are worthy to receive a portion of the relics of the Exalted One. Over the remains of the Exalted One, will we put up a sacred cairn and in their honour, will we celebrate a feast."[2]

The origin

1. *Tārānātha's Geschichte des Buddhismus in Indien*—translated into German by Anton Schiefner, pp. 9, 41, 146.

2. *Mahāparinibbāṇa Suttanta*—Translated by T. W. & C. A. F. Rhys Davids in *Dialogues of the Buddha*, Vol. III, p. 187.

Note. The original Pāli text here is also interesting and we quote it in *full*. (Bhagavā pi Khattiyo, Mayam pi Khattiyā. Mayam pi arahāma Bhagavato Sarīrānam bhāgam, mayam pi Bhagavato Sarīrānam thūpañca mahañ ca karissāmāti. Dīgha Nikāya, P. T. S. Vol II. (pp. 164—165)

Here we see that the claim of the Licchavis was based on the fact that they were Kṣatriyas or people of the same caste as the Divine Master ; hence they were entitled to a portion of the relics. Similar claims based on the same argument were forwarded also by Ajātaśatru, the powerful king of Magadha, who also sent a messenger with the message, "The Lord is a Kṣatriya and so am I. Therefore I deserve a share of the relics." The very same claim was preferred by the Bulis of Allakappa, the Koliyas of Rāmagāma, the Mallas of Pāvā and the Moriyas of Pipphalivana, all of whom advanced their right on the ground, "The Lord is a Kṣatriya and so are we," while the Śākyas of Kapilavastu claimed him as their very kin.[1] A Licchavi named Mahāli says, "I am a Khattiya, so is the Buddha. If his knowledge increases and he becomes all-knowing, why should it not happen to me."[2] It is apparent, therefore, that the "Licchavis were as good Kṣatriyas as Ajātaśatru of Magadha and the other Kṣatriya peoples in north-eastern India in Buddha's time. In the introduction to the Sigāla Jātaka, we read of a Licchavi girl, the daughter of a Kṣatriya and high-born."[3] Dr. Richard Fick in his well-known work, *The*

1. *Mahāparinibbāṇa Suttanta* in the Dīgha Nikāya, P. T. S. Vol. III, pp. 164-166.

2. *Sumangala Vilāsinī*, Pt. 1. P. T. S. p. 312.

3. 'Licchavi Kumārikā Khattiyadhītā Jātisampannā—Jātaka edited by V. Fausboll, Vol. II, p. 5.

Social Organisation in North-east India in Buddha's time, is rather sceptical as to whether the word Kṣatriya as used in the Pāli texts has exactly the same connotation as in the ancient Brāhmanical literature, while he has no such doubt with regard to the Brāhmaṇas. But as Professor Oldenberg observes, there is no ground for this scepticism. "When it is admitted," says this distinguished savant, "that the families of Goutama, Bhāradvāja etc. were all grouped together in the caste of Brāhmaṇas as being pervaded all of them by the mystic potency of the *Brahman,* I cannot see why just in the same way, and answering to exactly similar modes of expression in the texts, it should not be held that families like those of Śākyas, etc. all of whom felt in themselves the potency of the Kṣatra nobility, all of whom said, 'Mayaṃ pi khattiyā' are to be reckoned as belonging to a single caste of the Khattiyas (Kṣatriyas)—a single caste of which the members, when they said to each other 'I am a Khattiya,' 'I too am a Khattiya,' knew and acknowledged each other as persons of the same kind and nature."[1]

That the Licchavis were Kṣatriyas appears also from the Jaina sacred literature. Just as the Licchavis of Vaiśālī honoured the Buddha

1. Prof. H. Oldenberg, '*On the History of the Indian Caste System*' translated into English from the Z. D. M. G, Vol LI by Prof H. C. Chākladār, Ind. Ant, Vol. XLIX. Decem. 1920, p. 227.

at his death by erecting a noble monument (stūpa) over their shares of the remnants of his body so they had, before this, done honour to the memory of the great Mahāvīra, the founder of Jainism, at his death. The Jaina Kalpasūtra narrates: 'In that night in which the venerable ascetic Mahāvīra died, went off, quitted the world, cut asunder the ties of birth, old age, and death; became a Siddha, a Buddha, a Mukta, a maker of the end (to all misery), finally liberated, freed from all pains, the eighteen confederate kings of Kāśī and Kośala, the nine Mallakis and nine Licchavis, on the day of new moon, instituted an illumination on the poshadha, which was a fasting day; for they said, 'since the light of intelligence is gone, let us make an illumination of material matter.'[1] The Jaina works further tell us, as Professor Jacobi points out, that these nine Licchavis were tributary to Cetaka, king of Vaiśālī and maternal uncle of Mahāvīra[2] who was a Jñātri Kṣatriya of the Kāśyapa Gotra, as we read in the Kalpasūtra. "The venerable ascetic Mahāvīra belonged to the Kāśyapa gotra... The venerable ascetic Mahāvīra..., a Jñātri Kṣatriya, the son of a Jñātri Kṣatriya; the moon of the clan of the Jñātris; a Videha, the son of Videhadattā, a native of Videha, a prince

1. *Kalpa Sūtra* § 128 translated by Prof. H. Jacobi, S. B. E. Vol. XXII. P. 266.

2. Jacobi. op. cit. note I. p. 266.

of Videha",[1] and there are reasons to believe that Mahāvīra was a native of a suburb of Vaiśālī.[2] Mahāvīra's mother, Triśalā, is always styled as Kṣatriyāṇī, and the Licchavis, therefore, must have been Kṣatriyas. That the Licchavis were looked upon as persons of very high pedigree appears from a passage in another work of the Jaina sacred literature, the Sūtrakṛitāñga, where we read, "A Brāhmaṇa or Kṣatriya by birth, a scion of the Ugra race or a Licchavi, who enters the order eating alms given him by others, is not stuck up on account of his renowned Gotra."[3]

The Licchavis were Kṣatriyas of the Vāśiṣṭha gotra. In the account of the first meeting of the Buddha with the Licchavis as given in the Mahāvastu Avadāna, we read that the latter in order to avert a plague that was depopulating their town, brought the Master to Vaiśālī with great respect and honour, and the Buddha, when speaking to the Licchavis, always addressed them as Vāśiṣṭhas.[4] Again according to the Tibetan Dulva, when King Ajātaśatru of Magadha was leading an army against the Licchavis, these latter also

1. Jacobi op. cit. § 108-110., pp. 255-6.
2. Ibid, p. x-xii.
3. Jacobi, *Jaina Sūtras*, part II, S. B. E. Vol. XLV, p. 321.
4. "Licchavikā āhansu. Anyadāpi Bhagavan. Bhagavānāha, anyadāpi Vāsiṭṭhā. Bhūtapūrvaṁ Vāsiṭṭhā atītamadhvāne pāñcāle janapade Kaṁpillanagare Rājā Brahmadatto nāma rājyam kāresi "

Le Mahāvastu edited by E. Senart Vol. I. p. 283. The Licchavis are addressed as Vāśiṣṭhas many times in this account pp. 253-300.

made preparations to meet him ; and as they were starting out, they met Maudgalyāyana entering Vaiśāli to get alms. So they asked him whether they would be victorious. He answered them, "Men of Vaśiṣṭha's race, you will conquer."[1] Moreover the Jaina sacred works lay down definitely that Kṣatriyānî Trīśalā, the mother of Mahāvîra, was a sister of Ceṭaka, one of the kings of Vaiśālī, and belonged to the Vāśiṣṭha gotra (S. B. E. Vol. XXII, p. XII). We read in the Âyārāṅga Sūtra (11. I5. 15) : "The venerable ascetic Māhāvīra's father belonged to the Kāśyapa gotra ; he had three names, Siddhārtha, Sreyāṃsa, and Gasaṃsa. His mother belonged to the Vāśiṣṭha gotra, and had three names, Triśalā, Videhadattā and Priyakārinī."[2]

Thus we observe that, both according to the Buddhist and Jaina Canonical works, the Licchavis belonged to the Vāśiṣṭha gotra. In the Nepāl Vaṃśāvalī, the Licchavis have been allotted to the Sūryavaṃśa or solar race of the Kṣatriyas.[3] This is quite in agreement with the fact elicited from the Buddhist records that they were Vāśiṣṭhas by gotra, for we know from the Aitareya Brāhmaṇa that the gotra or pravara of a Kṣatriya is the same as that of his purohita or family priest, who makes him perform the

1. Rockhill, *Life of the Buddha*. p. 97. ff.
2. Jacobi, *Jaina Sūtras*, S. B. E. Vol. XXII pp xii and 193.
3. *Indian Antiguary*, Vol XXXVII, pp. 78-80.

sacrifices.[1] Sir R. G. Bhāndārkar also points out that the gotra of a Brāhmaṇa "could be assumed for sacrificial purposes by a Kṣatriya, for according to Aśvalāyana (Śr. S. XII .15.), the gotra and the ancestors invoked of the Kṣatriyas are those of their priests or chaplains, and the only Ṛṣi ancestors that all the Kṣatriyas have, are Mānava, Aila and Paurūravasa. The names of these do not distinguish one Kṣatriya family from another and, to answer the purposes of such a distinction, the gotra and ancestors of the priest are assumed."[2] The Vāśiṣṭha gotra was therefore the gotra of their family priest, and we know that the Vāśiṣṭhas were the family priests of the kings of the solar race, especially of the Ikshvākus ; there is thus an agreement between the Nepāl Vaṃśāvalī and the evidences from the Buddhist sources and the Jaina records also corroborate the same. As Professor Jacobi observes, "According to the Jainas, the Licchavis and the Mallakis were the chiefs of Kāśī and Kośala. They seem to have succeeded the Aiksvākas who ruled there in the times of the Rāmāyaṇa.[3] The Sanskrit epic tells us that the city of Vaiśālī was founded by Viśāla, a son of Ikshvāku and the heavenly nymph,

---

1. *Aitareya Brāhmaṇa, Ch.* 34, Kāṇḍa 7 verse 25.

2 Sir R. G. Bhāndārkar, *Vaiṣṇavism, Śaivism, and minor Religious Systems*. P. 12.

3. Jacobi, *Jaina Sūtras*, Part II, p. 321, note 3.

Alamvuṣā,[1] while the Viṣṇu Purāṇa substitutes Tṛṇaviṇdu, a later scion of the Ikṣvāku family as the father of the eponymous hero, who founded the city. This shows at least that at the time when these Brāhmanical Sanskrit books were composed, the ruling family of Vaiśālī was believed to have descended from the Ikṣvākus.

We may point out here that in the Mahāparinibbāṇa Suttanta, the Mallas of Kuśīnārā are addressed by the venerable Anuruddha and the venerable Ânanda as Vāseṭṭhas,[2] that is, Vāsiṣṭhas ; thus corroborating the Jaina account of the close connection of these two Kṣatriya tribes, both having the same gotra. In the Sangīti Sutta of the Dīgha-Nikāya, we find the Mallas of Pāvā also addressed as Vāseṭṭhas by the Buddha.[3] Their association with the Śākyas is also well-known. We read in the Karma-Śataka (a French translation of the Tibetan version of it, has been given by M. L. Feer) that Prabodha (Rab-sad), king of the Vṛjis, gave away his two daughters Māyā and Mahāmāyā, as brides to Śuddhodana, son of Simhahanu.[4] Besides, the Mahāvastu tells us of a contest at archery in which the Licchavi princes took part

1. *Rāmāyaṇa*, Bombay edition. Bālakāṇḍa, Ch. 47.
2. *Buddhist Suttas*, S B. E. Vol. XI. pp. 121-12?.
3 *Dialogues of the Buddha*, Part III, p. 202.
4. *Karma-Śataka*, 20. II. 7, Translated from Tibetan by M. L. Feer. Reprint. p. 40.

along with prince Siddhārtha.[1] Rockhill in his *Life of the Buddha* derived from Tibetan works, speaks of a tradition, according to which, the Śākyas and the Licchavis are branches of the same people. He refers to Sanang Setsen, who "in his History of the Eastern Mongols, p. 21, says that the Śākya race (to which the Buddha belonged) was divided into three parts, whose most celebrated representatives were Śākya the Great (the Buddha), Śākya the Licchavi, and Śākya the Mountaineer. Gnya Khri bstan po, the first Tibetan king, belonged to the family of Śākya the Licchavi".[2] The above legend is of very little historical value but it shows at least that the Śākyas and the Licchavis were considered to be allied races.

We have seen above the affinity of the Licchavis with the Mallas and the Śākyas.

Mythical accounts—Paramatthajotika on the Khuddakapatha and the Pujavaliya.

Now we come to the account of the mythical origin of the Licchavis, which can be gathered from Buddhaghosa's Paramatthajotikā on the Khuddakapāṭha.

There was an embryo in the womb of the chief queen of Benares. Being aware of it, she informed the king who performed the rites and ceremonies for the protection of it. With the embryo thus perfectly protected,

1. Senart, *Mahāvastu Avadāna*, Vol. II, p. 76.
2. Rockhill, *The Life of the Buddha* (popular edition) p. 203, note.

the queen entered the delivery chamber when it was fully mature. With ladies of great religious merit, the delivery took place at the dawn of day. A lump of flesh of the colour of lac and of bandhu and jīvaka flowers came out of her womb. Then the other queens thought that to tell the king that the chief queen was delivered of a mere lump of flesh while a son, resplendent like gold, was expected, would bring the displeasure of the king upon them all; therefore, they, out of fear of exciting displeasure of the king, put that lump of flesh into a casket, and after shutting it up, put the royal seal upon it, and placed it on the flowing water of the Ganges. As soon as it was abandoned, a god wishing to provide for its safety, wrote with a piece of good cinnabar on a slip of gold the words, "The child of the chief queen of the King of Benares" and tied it to the casket. Then he placed it on the flowing current of the Ganges at a place where there was no danger from aquatic monsters. At that time an ascetic was travelling along the shore of the Ganges close by a settlement of cowherds. When he came down to the Ganges in the morning, and saw a vessel coming on, he caught hold of it thinking that it contained rags (*pamsukula*), but seeing the tablet with the words written thereon and also the seal and mark of the King of Benares, he opened it and saw that piece of flesh. Seeing it, he thus thought within himself :—"It may be an embryo, and there is nothing stinking or putrid in it," and taking it to his hermitage, he placed it in a pure place. Then after half a month had passed, the lump broke up into two pieces of flesh ; the ascetic nursed them with still greater care. After the lapse of another half a month, each of the pieces of flesh developed fine pimples for the head and the two arms and legs. After half a month from that time, one of the pieces of flesh became a son resplendent like gold, and the other became a girl. The ascetic was filled with paternal affection for the babies and milk came out of his thumb. From that time forward, he obtained milk with rice ; the rice he ate himself and gave the babies the milk to drink. Whatever got into the stomach of these two infants looked as if put into a vessel of precious transparent stone (maṇi), so that they seemed to have no skin (nicchavi) ; others said : "The two (the skin and the thing in the stomach) are attached to each other (līnā-chavi) as if they were sewn up together" ; so that these infants owing to their being *nicchavi* i. e. having no skin, or on account of their being *Līnāchavi* i. e. attached skin or same skin, came to be designated as *Licchavis.* The ascetic having to nurse these two children had to enter the village in the early morning for alms and to return when the day was far advanced. The cowherds coming to know this conduct of his, told him, "Revered sir, it is a great trouble for an ascetic to nurse and bring up children; kindly make over the children to us, we shall nurse them, do you please attend to your own business".. The ascetic assented gladly to their proposal. On the next day, the cowherds levelled the road, scattered flowers, unfurled banners and came to the hermitage with music. The ascetic handed over the two children with these words: "The children are possessed of great virtue and goodness, bring them up with great care and when they are grown up, marry them to each other; please the king and getting a piece of land, measure out a city, and instal the prince there." "All right, sir," promised they, and taking away the children, they brought them up. The children, when grown up, used to beat with fists and kicks, the children of the cowherds whenever there was a quarrel in their sports. They cried and when asked by their parents, "Why do you cry?" They said, "These nurselings of the hermit, without father and mother, beat us very hard". Then the parents of these other children would say, "These children harass the others and trouble them, they are not to be kept, they must be abandoned. (*Vajjitabbā*)" Thenceforward that country measuring three hundred yojanas is called *Vajji*. Then the cowherds securing the goodwill and permission of the king, obtained that country, and measuring out a town there, they anointed the boy, king. After giving marriage of the boy, who was then sixteen years of age, with the girl, the king made it a rule : "No bride is to be brought in from the outside, nor is any girl from here to be given away to any one." The first time they had two children—a boy and a girl, and thus a couple of children was born to them for sixteen times. Then as these children were growing up, one couple after another, and there was no room in the city for their gardens, pleasure groves, residential houses and attendants, three walls were thrown up round the city at a distance of a quarter of a yojana from each other ; as the city was thus again and again made larger and still larger (Viśālikatā), it came to be called Veśālī. This is the history of Veśālī.[1]

Another mythical account—Pujavaliya.

The Pujāvaliya[2], a Ceylonese Buddhist work, also gives the same account though with some slight variations. These stories, of course, are entirely mythical and must have grown up in very recent times, there being no evidence in the sacred canon itself to corroborate any part of the

1. *Paramatthajotikā on the Khuddakapâṭha* edited by H. Smith, P. T. S, pp. 158-160.
2. Spence Hardy, *Manual of Buddhism*, 2nd edition, 1880, pp. 242-243.

narrative. It shows at least that the Licchavis were regarded as Kṣatriyas. The two derivations of the name, Licchavi, offered by Buddhaghosa in the above story, are no doubt entirely fanciful. Licchavi is the name of a race or tribe. The people must have acquired that name ages before they come to our notice in the pages of the Buddhist or Jaina literature, or in Kauṭilya's Arthaśāstra. Attempts at finding a derivation for the word are at best only ingenuous and are very likely to be fanciful. Buddhaghosa's derivations must have been invented in a late age when the Licchavis had acquired great renown and power, and it was found necessary to find out some meaning for the word which is rather peculiar and defies easy analysis by the ordinary rules of grammar. Hence they were associated with some myths, and we have the fanciful explanation given above. But it must be observed that the two derivations suggested by the great commentator are almost exactly the same as those given in Chinese Buddhist works. According to the Shan-hsien-lü (Chapter 8) the word "Licchavi" (or Lecchavi) is said to mean 'skin thin' or 'same skin,' the name being treated as a derivative of cchavi (chchhavi) which means 'skin'.[1] These are the same as

Derivations of the term 'Licchavi'

1. T. Watters, *On Yuan Chwang*, Vol. II, p. 77.

Buddhaghosa's *Nicchavi* or 'no skin', that is, 'thin skin' and 'lîna chavi' or 'joined skin,' that is, 'same skin'. This close agreement between the two sets of analysis and interpretation shows that both of them most probably drew materials from a common source.

The story recounted by Buddhaghosa on the authority of some Purāṇas, of which at present we know nothing, has no historical value, yet it is significant that even according to this account, the Licchavis were of Kṣatriya origin. There can be no doubt of this fact, and it is clear that at the time that the great Buddha and Mahāvīra lived and preached, the Licchavis were recognised as Kṣatriyas, who held their heads very high on account of their high birth and with whom the highest born princes of eastern India considered it an honour to enter into matrimonial alliance. We have seen how the great and powerful king Ajātaśatru was always designated by the family name of his mother in the Pāli Buddhist Tripiṭaka. Even two centuries later than the above two great preachers, at the time of Candragupta, the Licchavis were of equal rank and position with the great Kṣatriya peoples of Northern India, viz: the *Madras* in the west, the *Kuru-Pañcālas* in the central region, and the Mallas and others in the east—the tribes who were organised in corporations of warriors and lived upon their position as *rājās*, that is, as owners of land deriving an income from their tenants.

Coming down to the time when the present code of Manu was composed, we find that the Licchavis were still looked upon as Kṣatriyas but as Vrātya Kṣatriyas. Manu says that "from a Vrātya of the Kṣatriya caste sprang the Jhalla, the Malla, the Licchavi, the Naṭa, the Karaṇa, the Khasa, and the Drāviḍa."[1] (Manu S. x. 22.) and immediately before this, Manu takes care to tell us what he exactly means by the term Vrātya ; he says, "Those (sons) whom the twice-born beget on wives of equal caste, but who, not fulfilling their sacred duties, are excluded from the Sāvitrī, one must designate by the appellation Vrātyas."[2] (Manu S.x. 20.) The expression avratāḥ (not fulfilling their sacred duties) in the above verse, means, as Dr. Bühler points out[3], 'not being initiated at the proper time', on the authority of what Manu himself states in an earlier chapter, where he fixes the upper limits in the ages before which the initiation of the twice-born castes must take place. We read, "The (time for the) Sāvitrī (initiation) of a Brāhmaṇa does not pass until the completion of the sixteenth year (after conception), of a Kṣatriya until the

Licchavis in Manu's code.

1. Bühler, *Manu*, p. 406.
2. Ibid, op. cit. pp. 405-406.
3. Ibid, op. cit. pp. 405-406, note 20.

completion of the twenty-second and of a Vaiśya until the completion of the twenty-fourth. After those periods, men of these three castes who have not received the sacrament at the proper time, become Vrātyas (outcastes) excluded from the Sāvitrī (initiation) and despised by the Âryans."[1] Here, in the definition of the term Vrātya as well as the upper limit of the initiation, Manu is in agreement with the earlier lawgivers, Gautama, Âpastamba, Vaśiṣṭha and Baudhāyana.[2] Now from the passages of Manu quoted above, it will be seen that Manu states explicity that the Vrātya is a person whom a twice-born begets on a wife of equal caste and not on a wife of an inferior or of a superior caste, as is the case with the *Anulomas* and the *Pratilomas*, but the Vrātya is looked upon with disfavour by the orthodox people on account of his failure to get himself initiated at the appointed time. In the case of the Licchavis, therefore, there is no question that they were pure Kṣatriyas by origin, but what is averred about them is that they were not very careful in obeying the regulations about initiation and perhaps similar other matters, like the people in the Madhyadeśa,[3] the central region, where the Brahmanic form of faith prospered

1. Bühler, op. cit pp. 36-37
2. Gautama, XXI, 11, Apa. 1. 1 22 Vas XI 74-79 Baudh I. 16, 16
3. See Manu, II. 21

D

and continued in its pristine vigour. From what we know of the religious history of the Licchavis as a people, it is but natural to expect that they would fall off from the strict observance of the Brahmanic regulations. We have seen that Mahāvīra, the founder of Jainism, was of their very kin and most probably a fellow townsman and we also know that his followers were many among the residents of Vaiśālī, even among the higest officers as we see in the case of Sīha. Then again, the fact that the Licchavis as a people had won, as we shall see in the chapters that follow, the good graces of the great Buddha as well as of the followers of the religion preached by the Enlightened One, appears to have been predominant in the Licchavi country during the centuries that intervened between the origin of Buddhism and the advent of Manu whom Prof. Bühler would place in about 200 B.C.—200 A. D.[1] During this long interval when the two great heretic faiths flourished in their country, it is but natural to expect that the Licchavis were not very particular about initiation and similar other ceremonies and practices that were required to be performed by the regulations of the orthodox Brāhmins. Hence, we can very well understand how Manu, the great Brahmanical law-giver, came to dub the Licchavis as Vrātyas and we have seen how

1. Bühler, Manu, Introduction, p. CXVII

the author of this code has taken care to avoid any chance of misunderstanding the exact connotation of the term Vrātya. He had already defined it in the second chapter of his book, yet he explains it again and says specifically that the term does not imply any of the castes,—that a Vrātya is begot by a twice-born person on a wife of the same caste and hence the Licchavis were of pure Kṣatriya parentage on both sides. To claim the authority of this passage of Manu in support of a theory of non-Aryan origin of the Licchavis is quite unwarranted.

The above discussion, we hope, will also explain what the lexicographers and the author of the Vaijayantî[1] declare about the origin of the Licchavis, viz, that they were sons of a Kṣatriya Vrātya and a Kṣatriyā. They have, all of them, followed Manu and a separate discussion of their statements is unnecessary.

At the same time, however, it must be admitted that the Licchavis had not entirely fallen off from the Brahmanic society : in the fourth century A D., just as Ajātaśatru had gloried in the title of *Vedehiputto*, the son of a daughter of Videha people, that is, of the Licchavis who occupied the Videha country, so also it was considered a glory to an orthodox Gupta Emperor to have been a

1. The Vaijayantî, edited by Gustav Oppert, p. 76.

Licchavi-dauhitra or the son of a daughter of the Licchavis.

Dr. Fleet who has edited the inscriptions in which the Gupta-Licchavi connection is mentioned, observes, "Proof of friendly relations between the early Guptas and the Licchavis, at an early time, is given by the marriage of Candra Gupta I with Kumāra Devī, the daughter of a Licchavi or of a Licchavi king. And that the Licchavis were then at least of equal rank and power with the early Guptas, is shewn by the pride manifested by the latter in this alliance as exhibited in the record of names of Kumāra Devî, and of her father or of her family on some of the gold coins of Candra Gupta I, and by the uniform application of the epithet, 'daughter's son of a Licchavi' to Samudra Gupta in the geneological inscriptions.[1] Fleet even goes so far as to declare that in all probability the so-called Gupta era is a Licchavi era, dating either from a time when the republican or tribal constitution of the Licchavis was abolished in favour of a monarchy or from the commencement of the reign of Jayadeva I as the founder of a royal house in a branch of the tribe that had settled in Nepāl.[2] The fact that this royal house that was planted by the Licchavis in Nepāl about the period 330 to 355 A. D. by Jayadeva I[3] was all along Brahmanical,

1. J. *Fleet, Gupta Inscriptions—Corpus Ins. Ind.* Vol. III, Introduction, p. 155. 2. Ibid, p. 133 3 Ibid. p. 136.

proves that the Licchavis had not entirely dissociated themselves from the Brahmanic faith. We thus observe that the power and glory of the Licchavis during the period of Brahmanic revival under the Guptas were as great as under the Śiśunākas and the Mauryas and that their position as one of the leading and most honoured Kṣatriya families in Eastern India was fully recognised. Before leaving this question of origin, it remains for us to refer to the two theories about the Tibetan and Persian affinities of the Licchavis started by the late Drs. V. A. Smith and Satis ch. Vidyābhūsan respectively. Dr. Smith's conclusion

The late Dr. V. A. Smith's theory—the Tibetan origin.

about the Tibetan affinity rests on the agreement that is observed between the Tibetans and the Licchavis in the custom of exposure of the dead and in judicial procedure. We shall discuss these two points one by one. The prevalence among the Licchavis of the practice of exposing the dead to be devoured by wild animals is vouched for by a passage in *Beal's Romantic Legend of Śākya Buddha*[1] derived from Chinese sources. There we have the description of a visit paid by Bodhisatta (*Gautama*) to a cemetery at Vaiśālī where the Ṛṣis are stated to have answered his question thereanent. "In that place the corpses of men are exposed to be devoured by the

1. P. 159.

birds; and there also they collect and pile up the white bones of dead persons, as you perceive; they burn corpses there also, and preserve the bones in heaps. They hang dead bodies also from the trees; there are others buried there, such as have been slain or put to death by their relatives, dreading lest they should come to life again; whilst others are left there upon the ground that they may return, if possible, to their former homes." From this statement Dr. Smith argues, "whatever obscurity may exist in this passage, it certainly proves a belief that the ancient inhabitants of Vaiśālī disposed of their dead sometimes by exposure, sometimes by cremation, and sometimes by burial. The tradition is supported by discoveries made at prehistoric cemeteries in other parts of India, which disclose very various methods of disposing of the dead."[1] He then concludes from the similarity which these customs of the disposal of the dead bear with those of Tibet that the Licchavis had Tibetan affinities. But it may be observed that we need not go to Tibet for these customs, in as much as they were prevalent among the Vedic Aryans from whom the Licchavis' descended. We read in the well-known funeral hymn of the Atharva Veda (XVIII. 2. 34.),[2]

1. *Indian Antiquary*, 1903. p. 234.

2. "Ye nikhātā ye paroptā ye dagdhā ye coddhitāḥ sarvāṁstāngna āha pitrin haviṣe atiave."

Atharvaveda Saṁhitā edited by R. Roth and W. D. Whitney, p. 339.

"They that are buried, and they that are scattered (*reap*) away, they that are burned and they that are set up (*uddhita*)—all those Fathers, Oh Agni, bring thou to eat the oblation."[1] Prof. Whitney whose translation of the verse we have quoted here, observes on the expression *Uddhitās*, "It evidently refers to exposure on something elevated, such as is practised by many peoples."[2] Prof. Whitney also refers to an analogous passage in Âpastamba (I. 87.) where the divisions are (*Ye garbhe mamrus*), *parāstās*, *uddhitās* and *nikhātās*, so that there also we find a reference to the custom of burial and exposure on a raised platform (*Uddhitās*). Zimmer in his Altindisches Leben[3] thinks that in this passage there is "a parallel to the Iranian practice of casting out the dead to be devoured by beasts" though he takes the word *paroptās* in this sense, and explains *uddhitās* otherwise.[4] The Vedic literature shows that cremation was one of the methods of the disposal of the dead. The methods other than that of cremation were in vogue, it seems, in particular localities and among particular classes or peoples. It is evident, therefore, that the custom of exposure of the dead was not a practice unknown to the

---

1. *Atharva Saṁhitā* translated by W. D. Whitney and revised and edited by C. R. Lanman, Harvard. Or. Series, Vol. VIII. p. 840,
2. Ibid, p. 841.
3. p. 402
4. Macdonell and Keith, *Vedic Index*. Vol. I. p. 8.

Vedic Aryans but was apparently brought by them from their cradle into India in as much as we find the same to be the most approved method among the most closely allied branch of their family, viz, the Iranians. To seek for the origin of this ancient Aryan custom in Tibet is absolutely unwarranted. The other argument of Dr. Smith that the ancient judicial procedure at Vaiśālī as given in the Aṭṭhakathā, is substantially identical with the modern procedure at Lhāsā as observed by the Bengali traveller in Tibet, the late Rai Bahadur Sarat Chunder Das C. I. E., need not detain us very long. This procedure the Tibetans must have imbibed along with Buddhism from the province of Behār, which was nearest to their frontiers and which was inhabited by the descendants of the Licchavis of old.

The Late Dr. Vidyabhusan's theory-Persian Origin.

Dr. Satis Chandra Vidyābhuṣaṇ holds that they were of Persian origin. His strongest argument is the verbal coincidence between *Nisibis* in the Persian Empire and the fancied occurrence of the word *Nicchivi* in Manu. We have already demonstrated that it was a misreading for which Kulluka was responsible, and as such it offers no basis for building up a theory of Persian affinity for the Licchavis. Dr. Vidyābhūṣaṇ avers, "It appears to me very probable that while about 515 B. C. Darius, king of Persia, sent an expedition to India, or rather caused the Indus to be explored from the land of Pakhtu (Afghans) to its mouth, some of his Persian subjects in Nisibis (off Herat) immigrated to India, and having found the Punjab overpeopled with the orthodox Brāhmaṇas, came down as far as Magadha (Behar) which was at that time largely inhabited by Vrātyas or outcaste people."[1] This is absurd on the face of it. The Licchavis were already a flourishing people, long established in the Videha country and had built up a splendid capital at Vaiśālī at the time of Buddha's death ; and whether we take the date of this event to be 480. B. C. as the late Dr. V. A. Smith thinks, or what is more probable, to be 545. B. C., the traditional date maintained by the Ceylonese Buddhist monks, it is simply absurd to identify the Licchavis with the followers or subjects of Darius who were exploring the Indus about 515 B. C.

Beal's theory—yue-chi.

It remains for us to refer to another theory about the foreign origin of the Licchavis, started by Beal, viz., that they were 'yue-chi.'[2] It hardly requires to be refuted as the yue-chi came to India about the beginning of the christian era and

1. *Indian Antiquary*, 1908. p. 70.
2. *The Life of Hiuen Tsiang* by Beal, Intro. p. xxii.

the Licchavis were a highly civilised and prosperous people in the fifth and sixth centuries before Christ, when the Ephthalites or white Huns had not started from their original home in the east.

CHAPTER II.

Vaisali, the Capital of the Licchavis.

Vaiśālī, 'the large city' par excellence is renowned in Indian History as the capital of the Licchavi Rājās and the head quarters of the great and powerful Vajjiaṇ Confederacy.[1] This great city is intimately associated with the early history of both Jainism and Buddhism; it carries with itself the sacred memories of the founders of these two great faiths that evolved in north-eastern India, five hundred years before the birth of Christ. Vaiśālī claims the founder of Jainism as its own citizen. The Sūtrakṛitāṅga,[2] one of the Jaina canonical works, says about Mahāvīra, the last Tīrthaṅkara of the Jainas as follows: "Evaṃ se uḍāhu aṇuttaramaṇī aṇuttaradaṃsī anuttara-ñāṇadaṃsaṇadhare arahā Nāyaputte bhagavaṃ Vesālie Viyāhie (Vyākhyātavān) iti bemi." "Thus spoke the Arhat Jñātriputra, the reverend, famous native of Vaiśālī, who possessed

Its importance.

Vaisali and Mahavira.

1. Rhys Davids, Buddhist India, p. 40.
2. I. 2, 3. 22.

the highest knowledge and the highest faith, who possessed (simultaneously) the highest knowledge and faith."[1] This passage is also repeated in another Jaina work, the *Uttarādhyayanasūtra* with a slight variation.[2] Mahāvīra is spoken of as Vesālie or Vaiśālika i. e. a native of Vaiśālī.[3] Moreover Abhayadeva in his commentary on Bhagavatī 2, 1. 12, 2. explains Vaiśālika by Mahāvīra and speaks of Viśālā as Mahāvīrajananī or 'the mother of Mahāvīra.'[4] Besides, from a comparison of the Buddhist and Jaina Scriptures, it appears that Kuṇḍagrāma, the birthplace of Mahāvīra, was a suburb of Vaiśālī.[5] Mahāvīra's mother Triśalā was a sister to Ceṭaka, one of the so-called Rājās of that Licchavi city.[6] The Jaina Kalpasūtra speaks of the connection of Mahāvīra with the Videha country and its capital, Vaiśālī in these words: "The venerable ascetic Mahāvīra—a Videha, the son of Videhadattā, a native of Videha, a prince of Videha—had lived thirty years in Videha when his parents went to the world of the gods (i. e. died) and he with the permission of his elder brother and the authorities of the kingdom fulfilled his promise"[7] of

1. Jacobi, Jaina Sūtras, S. B. E. pt II. p. 261.
2. Ibid., pt II, Lecture VI. 17. p. 27.
3. Ibid., pt I. Introduction. XI.
4. Weber, *Indische Studien*, Band XVI, pp. 262-263.
5. Jacobi, *Jaina Sūtras* S. B. E. Vol. XXII, pp. X-XI.
6. Ibid p. XII.
7. Jacobi, Jaina Sūtras, p. 256, *Kalpa Sūtra*, §110.

going out to "establish the religion of the law which benefits all living beings in the whole universe."[1] During his later ascetic life also Mahāvīra did not neglect the city of his birth and we are told by the Kalpa Sūtra, that out of the forty two rainy seasons of this period of his life, he passed no less than twelve at Vaiśālī.[2]

Vaisali and the Buddha.

The connection of the Buddha with Vaiśālī is no less close and intimate. This city was hallowed by the dust of his feet early in his career and many of his immortal discourses were delivered here either at the mango-grove of Ambapālī, in the outskirts of the city or at Kuṭāgāraśālā in Mahāvana, the great forest stretching out up to the Himalayas. The Exalted One was charmed with the conduct of the Vajjis or Licchavis residing within the town and looked upon them with kindness and approbation. The seven points of excellence with which he charactised the Licchavis in answer to the queries put to him by the ministers sent by the King Ajātaśatru of Magadha are very well known ; we see there, how he spoke of the unimpeachable character of the people of Vaiśālī and tried to dissuade the Magadhan King from making fruitless attempts at robbing the people of that noble city of their independence. It is evident that the Enlightened One had a soft place in his heart for this mighty

1. Jacobi, Jaina Sūtras, Kalpa Sūtra § 111. 2. Ibid, § 122

and noble people and their splendid and extensive capital. And when at last the days of his earthly existence were drawing to a close, he paid a last visit to the city that had received his blessing and affection, the city that was always ready to honour and worship him, and as the Enlightened One felt within himself that the end was drawing nigh, that this was the very last view that he would ever have of this beautiful town, he cast a 'longing, lingering look behind'. In the words of the Mahāparinibbāṇa Suttanta, the Book of the Great Decease, "when the Exalted One had passed through Veśālī, and had eaten his meal and was returning from his alms-seeking, he gazed at Vesālī, with an elephant look,"[1] (that is, turning the whole body round as an elephant does, as Buddhaghosa explains), and then addressed the Venerable Ânanda, and said :—'This will be the last time, Ânanda, that the Tathāgata will behold Veśālī.'[2]

Vaisali and the Buddhist church

Even after the Enlightened One had entered into Nirvāṇa, Vaiśālī again drew to itself the care and attention of the whole Buddhist Church, but this time it was not on account of the many good qualities of character and powers of

1. Nāgāpalokitaṁ Veśāliyaṁ apaloketvā. (The Dialogues of the Buddha, pt. II, p. 131. f.)

2. English translation by T. W. and C. A. F. Rhys Davids, The Dialogues of the Buddha, pt. II, p. 131.

organisations of its citizens, but of the objectionable tenets held by the Vaiśālī monks who twisted and turned the noble precepts of the Great Preacher to suit their own convenience and to lead a life of less austerity and greater enjoyment of the good things of the earth than the Master permitted ; for example, they would have fresh meals even after the midday dinner and would accept gold and silver. The representatives of the entire congregation met at Vaiśālī itself and condemned in no equivocal terms the conduct of its pleasure-seeking Bhikṣus. This was the second general Council of the Buddhist Church.[1]

We have referred to a few only of the incidents connecting the great city of the Licchavis with the history of the growth and development of the Jain and Buddhist Churches ; there are innumerable references to the city and its people in both the literatures especially in the Buddhist Canon.

Foundation of Vaisali.

To the fanciful stories told by Buddhaghosa of the origin of the town, we have already referred in the previous chapter. We may, however, glean from them two outstanding facts that do not seem to admit of any doubt, viz, that the city was founded by the Licchavis and that the area covered by the town was very extensive ; in

1. Kern, *Manual of Buddhism*, pp. 103-109.

fact, it owes its name Vaiśālī to its being Viśāla or very large and wide in area. The great Kālidāsa has a pun on this name of the town when he speaks of "Śri-Viśālām Viśālām," or Viśālā, the immense town with immense prosperity. Vālmikī in the Bālakāṇḍa[1] of his Rāmāyaṇa tells us a story (to which we have already referred) of the foundation of the city different from that of Buddhaghosa. He says that it was founded by a son of Ikṣvāku and the heavenly nymph (Apsarā), Alambuṣā; after his name Viśāla, the city itself came to be called Viśālā. The Viṣṇupurāṇa says that it was Tṛṇavindu, who according to the geneological tree preserved in the Purāṇas, descended from Ikṣvāku and had by Alambuṣā a son named Viśāla.

The Visnu-purana Account.

The Rāmāyaṇa further tells us that when Rāma and his brother Lakṣmaṇa, guided by the sage Viśwāmitra, crossed the sacred river Ganges and reached its northern shore, on their way to Mithilā, the capital of the royal sage, Janaka, they had a view of the city of Vaiśālī. It does not tell us that it was exactly on the bank of the river, but it says that "while seated on the northern shore they saw the town."[2] It might be that the distant

The Ramayana Account.

1. Chap. 47.
2. Rāmāyaṇa (Bombay Edition) chap. 45. Verse. 9.

towers or the pinnacles of the temples met their gaze as they cast their glance northwards. Then the Rāmāyaṇa story continues, the eminent travellers went to the city of Viśāla which was an excellent town (Uttamā Purī), "charming and heavenly, in fact a veritable svarga."[1] Viśwāmitra, the guide, narrates here a fairly long mythological account to show the importance of the locality where Indra himself had sojourned for about a thousand years. Then the Ṛṣi goes on to say that the Ikṣvāku prince ruling over the country at the time was Sumati by name, and adds that by favour of Ikṣvāku, the father of the eponymous founder of the city and the ruling dynasty, all the kings of Vaiśālī (sarve vaiśālikā nṛpāḥ) were long lived, great souled, possessed of strength and power and highly virtuous.[2] One may very well question whether the author of the Rāmāyaṇa has here an overt allusion to the Rājās of Vaiśālī in the phrase 'vaiśālikā nṛpāḥ. From all the mythical stories above referred to, it is apparent that the name of the city had something to do with viśāla or extensive in area and from what we read of the description of the ruins that Yuan Chwang saw in the seventh century after Christ, there can hardly be any doubt of its wide extent. The Chinese traveller relates,

---

1. *Rāmāyaṇa* (Bombay Ed.) chap. 45 v. 11 & 12.
2. *Rāmāyaṇa* (Bombay Ed.) Ch. 47.

Yuan Chwang's Account.

"The foundations of the old city Vaiśālī were sixty or seventy li in circuit and the "palace-city" (i. e., the walled part of the city) was four or five li in circuit."[1] This would mean an area of about twenty miles in circumference for the outer town and the "Palace-city" of Yuan Chwang perhaps represents the earliest of the three cities which according to Buddhaghosa, was built to accommodate the Licchavis as they were growing rather fast; but its area would not in that case agree with the statement that each of the three walls was at a distance of a gāvuta (gavyūti) or a quarter yojana, that is roughly a league from the other. The description of Buddhaghosa is also supported by *Jātakaṭṭhakathā* to Ekapaṇṇa Jātaka where we are told:

The Jataka Account.

"At the time of the Buddha, the city of Veśālī was encompassed by three walls at a distance of a gāvuta from one another and that at three places there were gates with watch-towers and buildings (gopura-ṭṭā-lokayutaṃ)."[2] The three walls are adverted to in the Aṭṭhakathā to Lomahaṃsa Jātaka also.[3] The Tibetan Dulva iii f. 80, gives the following description. "There were three

Dulva Account

1. Watters, on Yuan Chwang, vol. II, p. 63.
2. Jâtaka (Fausboll), Vol. I. p. 504.
3 Ibid., Vol. I. p 389.

districts in Vaiśālī. In the first district were 7,000 houses with golden towers, in the middle district were 14,000 houses with silver towers, and in the last district were 21,000 houses with copper towers ; in these lived the upper, the middle and the lower classes according to their positions."[1] Dr. Hoernle in his English translation of the Jaina work, *Uvāsagadasāo*, advances the suggestion that the three districts here referred to in the Dulva and in the Aṭṭhakathā "may very well have been Veśālī proper, Kuṇḍapura and Vāṇiyagāma, occupying respectively the south-eastern, north-eastern and western portions of the area of the total city. Beyond Kuṇḍapura, in a further north-easterly direction lay the suburb (or 'station,' *sannivesa*) of Kollāga (see § 7) which appears to have been principally inhabited by the Kṣatriyas of the Nāya (or Jñātri) clan, to which Mahāvīra himself belonged ; for in § 66 it is described as the Nāya-kula."[2] Dr. Hoernle further observes that the phrases used in the Âyāraṅga Sutta like "Uttara-Khattiya-Kuṇḍapura-sannivesa or dahiṇa-māhaṇa-kuṇḍapura-sannivesa," "do not mean the northern Kṣatriya (resp. Southern Brahmanical) part of the place Kuṇḍapura, but the northern Kṣatriya etc., suburb of Kuṇḍapura

Dr. Hoernle's theory—Vaisali and Suburbs

1. Rockhill, *Life of the Buddha*, p. 62.
2. Hoernle, Uvāsagadasāo, Vol. II, Translation, Note 8, p. 4.

i, e, that suburb (Sannivesa) of the city of Kuṇḍapura, which lay towards the north and was inhabited by the (Nāya clan of) Kṣatriyas ; it was distinguished from the southern suburb of the same city (Kuṇḍapura or Veśālī) which was inhabited by the Brāhmins. This interpretation is confirmed by the parallel phrases in Kap. § 22. (*et passim*), Khattiya-Kuṇḍagāme Nayare and Māhaṇa-Kuṇḍagāme Nayare, which are rightly translated by the Kṣatriya (resp. the Brahmanical) part of the town Kuṇḍagāma."[1] He also points out that "the phrase ucca-nīya majjhimāiṃ kulāiṃ, 'upper, lower and middle classes' applied to the town of Vāṇiyagāma in sections 77, 78 (of the *Uvāsagadasāo*) curiously agrees with the description of Veśālī given in the Dulva."[2] The passage in the *Uvāsagadasāo* above referred to is the one in which Goyama, the senior disciple of Mahāvīra, addressed him thus : "I desire, Reverend Sir, with your permission, as the turn for the indulgence of my sixth meal has arrived, to go round the city of Vāṇiyagāma, to the upper, lower and middle classes, on a begging tour of house to house collection."[3]

The great founder of the rival faith of Buddhism must have paid many visits to the Licchavi capital and the reports of at least two

1. Hoernle, Uvāsagadasāo, p. 5.
2. Hoernle, Uvāsagadasāo, Vol. II. Translation, p. 6.
3. Ibid, p. 52,

besides that already referred to, are preserved in the Buddhist books. The earliest of his visits has been described at length in the Mahāvastu.[1] We are told there, how the people of Vaiśālī were troubled by a frightful pestilence which was laying their country waste and how they found all their efforts to stay the desolating plague entirely fruitless and in their dire distress sent to various holymen of great renown who failed to afford them any relief and as a last resort they sought the help of the Enlightened One who resided at the time at Rājagṛha, the Magadhan capital. The people of Vaiśālī sent a deputation headed by Tomara, a Licchavi chief of power and position, and at the same time of great learning, to Rājagṛha to bring the Exalted One to their city. Tomara went to Rājagṛha, fell down at his feet and sought his help with supplications, but was asked to apply to the King Śreṇika Bimbisāra who insisted on the condition that the Licchavis must welcome the Buddha at the border of their own dominions and that he himself would follow the great teacher to the boundaries of his own territory. To this the Licchavis readily assented and Bimbisāra secured the consent of the Buddha to save the Licchavis from the decimating disease.

The Magadhan king to impress the Licchavis

1. *Le Mahāvastu*, Ed. by E. Senart, Vol. I. p. 253. ff.

with an idea of his power and opulence, had the road all the way from Rājagṛha to the Ganges, which formed the boundary between the two dominions, levelled, rendered clean like the palm of the hand, decorated with flags, garlands and richly embroidered cloth; besides, the whole road was watered, flowers were freely scattered upon it and the smoke of rich incense perfumed its whole length. He himself followed the Enlightened One with his whole court and numerous retinue. The Licchavis both the *Abhyantara-Vaiśālakas*, the Vaiśālī-cockneys proper, living within the walls of the city and the *Bāhira-Vaiśālakas*, the people living in the outer town—the suburbs and surroundings—came in all their splendour and magnificience in all the glory of their dazzling garments, blue, purple, green, yellow, brown and crimson; their appearance as they approached was so splendid and ravishing that even the Great Buddha was impressed with the sight and said addressing the monks, "Bhikshus, you have never before beheld the Trayastviṃsa gods as they go out of their city Sudarśanā to the garden. Behold now the Licchavis of Vaiśālī who equal those gods in their prosperity and splendour. Look at the Licchavis with their elephants, with umbrellas of gold, their gold-covered litters, their chariots decorated with gold. See how they all come, both the young and the aged, as also those of middle age-all with ornaments on, with garments dyed crimson with lac and advancing with various beautiful movements." The Licchavis of Vaiśālī decorated the road from the Ganges to Vaiśālī with a magnificence that left the preparations made by the Magadhan king far behind, they provided for the comfort of the Exalted One and the congregation of monks on a still more lavish scale. As soon as the Enlightened One crossed over to the northern side of the river and stepped on the Licchavi soil, all malign influences that had hung over the country and were making a havoc among the people, vanished, and the sick and the suffering were restored to health. The Licchavis received him with all honour and reverence and guided him to their city, by easy stages with all the comfort and convenience that they were able to provide for him. Entering the city, the Enlightened One uttered the Svastyana-gāthā, the song of welfare, or according to the Pāli scriptures, the Ratana Sutta; they asked him whether he would live among the people of inner Vaiśālī or of outer Vaiśālī. The Exalted One would not live among either of them, but he accepted the invitation[1] of Bhagavatī Gośṛṅgī in the Mahāvana, the great forest extending from

1. Le Mahāvastu, Ed. by Senart, vol. I., pp 295—299.

their city far away to the north. The Licchavis who wished that the Exalted One might be induced to live in their city, built the Kūṭāgāraśālā, the peaked monastery, for him in the forest and paid their respects to him there. They offered it to him and the Buddhist congregation and he permitted the Bhikṣus to reside there. One day the Licchavis on coming to the Mahāvana learnt that the Exalted One had repaired to the Cāpāla-Caitya for spending the day; they proceeded there and presented it to him and the congregation of the śrāvakas or Buddhist monks. Similarly finding the Enlightened One spending the day at the Saptāmra-Caitya, the Bahuputra-Caitya, the Gautama-Caitya, the Kapinahya-Caitya and the Markaṭahrada-tīra-Caitya; the Licchavis made a gift of all these places of worship to the Exalted One and the Buddhist Church. Next, the courtesan, (gaṇikā) Âmrapālī made a gift of her extensive mango-grove to the congregation and similarly Bālikā made over Bālikā-chavi[1] which is evidently the same as the *Bālikārāma* in the Pāli Buddhist books.[2] On this visit to their city, the Enlightened One delivered many discourses to the people

Dedication of Kutagarasala

Shrines dedicated to the Buddha and the Buddhist Church

1. Le Mahāvastu, Ed. by Senart, p. 300.
2. *Vinaya Texts*, S. B. E. Vol. III, p. 408.

of Vaiśalī and established the Buddhist faith on a strong foundation at the capital of the Licchavis as he had already done at Rājagṛha, the capital of their rivals, the Magadhas.

Buddhist faith established

A similar account differing in slight details is given by Buddhaghosa in the introduction to his commentary on the Ratana-Sutta. He says that Vaiśālī was suffering from three troubles—famine, pestilence and sprites. We read in the Buddhist books of many occasions when the Enlightened One paid visits to Vaiśālī in the course of his peregrinations. The Mahāvagga tells us of an occasion when the Blessed One on his way from Rājagṛha to Vaiśālī noticed Bhikṣus with a superfluity of dress, 'almost smothered up in robes,' going along with their robes made up into a roll on their heads, or on their backs or on their waists. The Blessed One stayed on that occasion at the Gotamaka Caitya ; it was winter, the time between the Aṣṭakā festivals when the snow was falling and the Blessed One determined, by personal experience, the least quantity of robes that would suffice for keeping off the cold and preached accordingly to the Bhikshus.[1]

Buddha's discourse.

The Cullavagga[2] speaks of another occasion

1. *Vinaya Texts*, pt. II, S. B. E. pp. 210 & 211.
2. Ibid, pt. III, S. B. E. p. 101.

when the Blessed One lodged in the Kūṭāgāra Hall in the Mahāvana and the water being unfit for drinking, the use of strainers and filters was permitted for the Bhikṣus. This time, the Bhikṣus partaking freely of the abundant store of sweets offered by the laity, fell ill and were cured by the advice of Jīvaka Komārabhacca, the great physician. The sojourn of the Buddha on this occasion appears to have been rather long and the great teacher taught the Bhikṣus many matters connected with the sort of houses they were to build and live in; and this time also the Blessed One ordered the saṃgha to turn down the bowl as regards Vaddha, the Licchavi, who had brought a false charge against one of the brotherhood but afterwards relented on Vaddha again making due reparations. The Cullavagga tells us of another visit when the Blessed One stayed in the Kūṭāgāraśālā in the Mahāvana and spoke on the conduct of the Bhikṣus with regard to the building of new houses for the use of the order.

His advice.

We read of the Buddha coming down to Vaiśālī from Kapilavastu and staying there at the Kūṭāgāra Hall in the Mahāvana. This was the great occasion when Mahāpajāpatī Gotamī, the foster mother of the Blessed One, came with a number of Śākya ladies from Kapilavastu and through the intercession of Ânanda, obtained permission for women 'to go forth from the household life and enter the homeless state under the doctrine and discipline proclaimed by the Tathāgata.'[1]

From the accounts that we get from the Buddhist books whether Pāli or Sanskrit, we observe that Vaiśālī is represented as a town that was rich and prosperous. The Mahāvagga, one of the oldest books of the Pāli Canon, tells us that at the time the Buddha lived, Vaiśālī "was an opulent, prosperous town, populous, crowded with people, abundant with food ; there were seven thousand seven hundred and seven storeyed buildings, and seven thousand seven hundred and seven pinnacled buildings, and seven thousand seven hundred and seven pleasure grounds (ārāmas) and seven thousand seven hundred and seven lotus-ponds."[2]

Vaisali—rich and prosperous

A similar account of the prosperity of Vaiśālī is given in the Lalitavistara when the gods in the Tuṣita heaven were holding a discussion with regard to the family that would be the most suitable for the Bodhisattva to be born in. Some of the Tuṣita gods, the *devaputras* in advancing the claims of Vaiśālī for this great honour said, "This great city of Vaiśālī is prosperous and proud, happy and rich with abundant food, charming and delightful, crowded with many and various people, adorned

1. Vinaya texts, pt, III, p. 322.
2. Vinaya texts, pt, II, p. 171.

with buildings of every description, with storeyed mansions, buildings with towers, and palaces, with noble gateways and charming with beds of flowers in her numerous gardens and groves. This resembling the city of the gods is indeed fit for the birth of the Bodhisattva." This recommendation was not accepted on other grounds, but the passage speaks of the splendour and prosperity of the capital of the Licchavis. It was a prosperous and gay city, full of music.[1]

We next come to the accounts of the city left by the Chinese travellers of whom Fā-Hien visited it at the beginning of the fifth century A. D., that is, about a thousand years after the time the Buddha lived and delivered his discourses. Fā-Hien[2] says, "North of the city so named is a large forest, having in it the double-galleried vihāra where Buddha dwelt and the tope over half the body of Ânanda." The double-galleried vihāra is evidently the Kūṭāgāraśālā in the Mahāvana which stretched right up to the Himalayas as Buddhaghosa explains in his Sumaṅgalavilāsinī to the Mahāli Sutta in the Dīgha-Nikāya; in commenting upon the word "Mahāvana," he says, "outside the town lying in one stretch up to the Himalayas, there is a

Fa Hien's Visit.

Mahavana.

Buddhaghosa on Mahavana.

1. Fausboll, *Dhammapada* (Old Edition). p. 391.
2. Legge, *Fā-Hien*, p. 72.

natural forest which on account of the large area covered by it is called Mahāvana."[1] ("Bahinagare Himavantena saddhim ekābaddhaṃ hutvā ṭhitaṃ sayañ-jāta-vanaṃ atthi, yaṃ mahantabhāvena Mahāvanaṃ ti vuccati.") Legge remarks on the above quoted description given by Fā-Hien of the Kūṭāgāra-Vihāra, "it is difficult to tell what was the peculiar form of this Vihāra from which it got its name; something about the construction of its door, or cupboards, or galleries."[2] Here also Buddhaghosa offers a comment explaining the origin of the name. "In that forest was established a saṃghārāma or monastery. A pāsāda or a storeyed building was built on pillars and putting a pinnacle above, it was made into a kuṭāgārasālā resembling a chariot of gods (devavimāna). From it, all saṃghārāmas or monasteries are known as Kūṭāgārasālās."[3] This agrees with the description of the double-galleried vihāra, given by Fā-Hien. The upper storey was evidently built upon a large number of pillars instead of walls and on the top there was a peak or kūṭa, so that there were two galleries, one below and the other above, and from the upper storey rose a pinnacle as we see in the vimānas or rathas referred to by Buddhaghosa.

1. *Sumaṅgalavilāsinī*, pt. I (P. T. S) p 309.
2. Legge, *Fā-Hien*, p 72, *Note D.*
3. *Sumaṅgalavilāsinī*, pt. I. (P. T. S.) p. 309.

Yuan Chwang who visited the city more than two hundred years after Fā-Hien, found this great vihāra in ruins. "To the east of the tope of the Jātaka narrative," the pilgrim continues, "was a wonder-working tope on the old foundations of the 'two storeyed Preaching Hall' in which Ju-lai delivered the P'u-mên-to-lo-ni and other sūtras."[1] The "two-storeyed Preaching Hall" is no doubt the Kūṭāgāra Hall of two storeys as described by Buddhaghosa and as spoken of by Fā-Hien. This is also evident from what Yuan Chwang says immediately after the above passage. "Close to the remains of the Preaching Hall," the pilgrim says, "was the tope which contained the half-body relics of Ânanda."[2] This story of the Parinirvāṇa of Ânanda and the division of the remnants of the body has been told by Fā-Hien and the same account is also given in the Tibetan works. Fā-Hien narrates—"When Ânanda was going from Magadha to Vaiśālī, wishing his parinirvāṇa to take place (there), the devas informed King Ajātaśatru of it and the king immediately pursued him, in his own grand carriage, with a body of soldiers and reached the river. (On the other hand), the Licchavis of Vaiśālī had heard that Ânanda was coming (to their city), and they

1. Watters, On Yuan Chwang, Vol. II., p. 71.
2. Ibid., p. 71.

on their part came to meet him. (In this way), they all arrived together at the river, and Ânanda considered that, if he went forward, King Ajātaśatru would be very angry, while if he went back, the Licchavis would resent his conduct. He thereupon in the very middle of the river burnt his body in a fiery ecstacy of samādhi, and his parinirvāṇa was attained. He divided his body (also) into two, (leaving) the half of it on each bank ; so that each of the two kings got one half as a (sacred) relic, and took it back (to his own capital) and there raised a tope over it."[1]

Yuan Chwang's account of the Vṛji country of which Vaiśālī was the capital, agrees pretty well with the tradition of its prosperity preserved in the Buddhist Books. We read, "The Vaiśālī country is described by the pilgrim as being above 5,000 li in circuit, a very fertile region abounding in mangoes, plantains and other fruits. The people were honest, fond of good works, esteemers of learning, and orthodox and heterodox in faith."

Yuan Chwang's account

In the Tibetan works, a similar account is given of the prosperity and opulence of Vaiśālī which is invariably described in the Dulva as a kind of earthly paradise, with its handsome buildings, its parks

Tibetan account.

1. Legge, Fā-Hien, pp. 75-77.

and gardens, the singing birds and continual festivities among the Licchavis. "Nanda, Upānanda !" exclaimed the Chabbaggiyā Bhikshus when they visited Vaiśālī, "the Blessed One never saw the like of this, even when he was among the Trayastriṃcat devas." (Dulva X. f. 2.)[1] The *Romantic Legend of Śākya Buddha*[2] translated by Beal from Chinese sources, gives an account similar to that in the Lalita Vistara.[3] Here we read of a god in the Tuṣita heaven who speaks thus, "This Vajora country has a city called Vaiśālī, rich in every kind of produce; the people in peace and contentment; the country enriched and beautiful as a heavenly mansion; the king called 'Drumarāja'; his son without the least stain on his scutcheon; the king's treasuries full of gems, and gold and silver; perhaps you will be born there."

Chinese account of Vaisali.

The identification of Vaiśālī, the capital of the Licchavis, had long been a point of discussion among scholars. General Cunningham with his immense knowledge of the country and of the Buddhist literature, identified the present village of Basarh in the Muzafferpur district

Identification of Vaisali.

1. Rockhill, Life of the Buddha, p. 63.
2. P. 28.
3. Ed. by Dr. S. Lefmann. Vol. I. Text. p 21.

in Tirhut as marking the spot where stood Vaiśālī in ancient days[1] and M. Vivien de Saint Martin agreed with him, but the evidence that led Cunningham to arrive at this conclusion was not put forward with such fulness or clearness as the question certainly deserved; so that scholars had doubts as regards the identity. Prof. Rhys Davids says that the site was quite uncertain and that the site of Vaiśālī had still to be looked for somewhere in Tirhut.[2] Dr. W. Hoey sought to establish the identity, though on very insufficient evidence, of Vaiśālī with a place called Cherānd in the Chāprā or Sārān district. "Cherānd stands on the northern bank of the Ganges, in approximately N. lat. 25° 41 and E. long. 84° 55, about seven miles south from Chāprā."[3] This identification has been proved to be entirely untenable by Dr. V. A. Smith in his paper on Vaiśālī[4] from which we have quoted above; and he has succeeded in establishing that the identification by Cunningham of the village of Basarh with Vaiśālī admits of no doubt. This identity has been proved still more decisively by the Archæological explorations carried on in 1903-04 by Dr. T. Bloch on the site. Dr. Bloch excavated a mound called *Rājā Viśāl kā*

1. *Arch. S. Report*, Vol. 1, pp 55, 56 and Vol. XVI, p. 6
2. Rhys Davids, *Buddhist India*, p. 41.
3. J. A. S. B, 1900, Vol. LXIX, pt. 1, pp. 78, 83.
4. Dr. V. A. Smith, J. R. A. S, 1902, p. 267, n. 3.

garh and only eight trial pits were sunk. This was very insufficient considering the importance of the place. Three distinct strata have been found—the uppermost belonging to the period of Mahomedan occupation of the place, the second at a depth of about five feet from the surface, related to the epoch of the Imperial Guptas and the third at a still greater depth, belonging to an ancient period of which no definite date could be obtained, it being "represented only by a few scattered fragments, too scanty to offer any conclusive evidence as to their precise date or character."[1] The finds in the second stratum, however, are of very great value, specially the find in one of the small chambers of "a hoard of seven hundred clay seals evidently used as attachments to letters or other literary documents. They belonged partly to officials, partly to private persons, generally merchants or bankers, but one specimen bearing the figure of a liṅga with a triśūla on either side and the legend 'Âmrātakeśvara' evidently belonged to a temple."[2]

The names of certain Gupta kings, queens and princes on some of these seals, coupled with palæographic evidence, clearly demonstrate that they belonged to the fourth

1. Sir John H. Marshall, *Arch. Surv. of India*, Annual Report, 1903-04, p. 74.

2. *Ibid.* p., 74.

Rājā Viśāl Kā garh.

and fifth centuries after Christ when the Imperial Guptas were on the throne.[1] Some of the impressions show that the name Tīrabhukti (the original form of Tirhut) was applied to the province even in those early times and some show the name of the town itself, Vaiśālī. One of the clay-seals of a circular area, shows a female standing in a flower group with two attendants and two horizontal lines below reading (1) [Vai] Śālyām-araprakṛti-[Ku]-(2) tuṃbinā [m]—"Seal of the householders of...... at Vaiśālī."[2] Another seal also appears to have a similar legend. These things go to prove the identity of the site with Vaiśālī and there seems to be no ground to question this conclusion any longer. But it must be noted that the results so far obtained by excavations are very meagre, and it is a great pity that the Archæological Department had to give up the explorations for shortness of funds. We know not what invaluable materials for the history of India might lie buried under the earth in the mounds of Basarh as at other ancient sites in India.

---

1. Sir John H. Marshall, Arch. Surv. of India, Annual Report, 1903-04, p. 110.

2. Ibid., p. 110.

CHAPTER III.

Manners and Customs.

We have seen that the Licchavis were included in the great Vajjian Confederacy that dominated over the Vajji or Vṛji country. But sometimes Vajji and Licchavi were used indiscriminately as synonyms. At the time that Buddha lived, "the Vajjis were divided into several clans such as the Licchavis, the Vaidehis, the Tirabhuktis and so on and the exact number of these clans would appear to have been eight as criminials were arranged before the Aṭṭhakūlakā or eight clans which would appear to have been a jury composed of one member from each of the separate divisions of the tribe."[1] All these Vajjis lived in great amity and concord which was a particular mark of their confederacy and this union coupled with their martial instincts and the efficiency of their martial institutions made them great and powerful amongst the nations of north-eastern India.[2] Their sympathy for one another was exemplary. If a Licchavi fell ill, the other Licchavis came

Vajji and Licchavi losely used as synonyms.

Classification of Vajjian confederacy.

The people—sympathetic.

---

1. Cunningham, *Ancient Geography of India*, p. 447.

2. *Buddhist Suttas*, S. B. E. Vol. XI, p. 3 ; Vide also Turnour, *Pāli Buddhistical Annals*, No. 5, J. A. S. B. Dec. 1838, p. 992.

to see him. The whole clan would join any auspicious ceremony performed in the house of a Licchavi; if any foreigner of rank and power paid a visit to the Licchavi capital, they would all go out in a body to receive him and do him honour.[1] The young Licchavis were very handsome in appearance and very fond of brilliant colours in their dress and equipages.[2] The Buddha on his first meeting with the Licchavi nobles in their gay attire and rich and splendid equipages of various colours, was led to compare them to Tāvatiṃsa gods. A similar account we get from the Mahāparinibbāṇa Sutta, when the Licchavi nobles went out for the last time to meet the Blessed one as soon as they learnt that he had arrived at Vaiśālī and was staying at the mango-grove of Ambapālī in the outskirts of their city. "Ordering a number of magnificient carriages to be made ready, they mounted them and proceeded with their train to Vesālī. Some of them were dark,[3] dark in colour and wearing dark clothes and ornaments; some of them were fair, fair in colour, and wearing light clothes and ornaments; some of them were red, ruddy in colour, and

Beautiful in appearance

Love for Colours.

1. *Sumaṅgala Vilāsinī* (Burmese Edition) pp. 103—105

2. Watters, On Yuan Chwang, Vol. II. p. 79.

3. Nīla (Dīgha Nikāya, Vol II. p. 96) has been translated as "dark" by Prof. Rhys Davids; though for the complexion this may be a fair rendering, it is not so for the attire and the equipage.

wearing red clothes and ornaments; some of them were white, pale in colour, and wearing white clothes and ornaments."[1]

Exactly the same description of the colours favoured by the Licchavis is given in the Aṅguttara-Nikāya,[2] which shows that the Licchavis wore these colours not only on great festive occasions but in their ordinary daily life also. Once while the Enlightened One was staying at the Kuṭāgārasālā in the Mahāvana, five hundred of the Licchavis were seated round him doing obeisance. Some of them were nīla or blue all over in clothes and ornaments and similarly others were yellow, red or white. We may compare these descriptions with the more detailed accouut in the Mahāvastu of the colours preferred by the Licchavis. Thus says the Sanskrit Buddhist work: "There are Licchavis with blue horses, blue chariots, blue reins and whips, blue sticks, blue clothes, blue ornaments; blue turbans, blue umbrellas and with blue sword, blue jewels, blue footwear and blue everything befitting their youth"[3] and here the Mahāvastu quotes a verse, apparently from an older work or a traditional saying. In the very same terms the Mahāvastu

---

1 Buddhist Suttas, S. B. E. Vol. XI. p. 31.

2. Aṅguttara Nikāya P. T. S. part III., P. 239.

3. *Mahāvastu,* Vol. I., P. 259, for the text. The author is responsible for the English translation.

speaks of the Licchavis decked all in yellow (pīta) and in light red, the colour of the Bengal madder (mañjiṣṭha), in red (lohita), in white (śveta), in green (harita), and some in variegated colours (vyāyukta).[1] Perhaps the Licchavis were divided into separate clans, as Senart suggested, by the colour worn by each; otherwise it is difficult to explain why the same colour should be preferred for trappings of the horses, decorations of their carriages, as well as the articles of dress adorning their own persons. There was moreover a profusion of gold and jewels in everything in their equipage—carriages drawn by horses, gold-bedecked elephants, palanquins of gold set with all kinds of precious stones. Altogether there went out of the city of Veśālī twice 84,000 conveyances decked in pearl and gold, with all the wealth and splendour of kings. (rājaṛddhiye and samṛddhiye).

Classification of the Licchavis by Colour.

Display of their pomp and grandeur

All this speaks of a people who were greatly prosperous and in affluent circumstances; and it may be expected that they would be given to luxury and indolence. But this was not their character at the time when Buddha lived and

1. We have here followed the interpretation, suggested by Senart, of *Vyāyukta* (vide *Mahāvastu* note p. 574); this meaning however is very doubtful.

preached among them. The Saṃyutta Nikāya preserves a saying of Exalted One : "Look ye Bhikkhus here, how these Licchavis live sleeping with logs of wood as pillows, strenuous and diligent, (appamattā) zealous and active (ātāpino) in archery. Ajātaśatru, Vedehiputto, the Magadhan king, can find no defect in them, nor can he discover any cause of action (against them). Should the Licchavis, Oh Bhikkhus, in the time to come, be very delicate, tender and soft in their arms and legs, should they sleep in ease and comfort on cushions of the finest cotton up till the sun is up in the heavens, then the Magadhan king, Ajātaśatru, Vedehiputto, will find defects and will discover cause of action."[1] This testimony of the Buddha goes to show that the Licchavis were hardy and active, ardent and strenuous in their military training, so that their enemies could have no chance of getting them at a disadvantage.

Their character as depicted by the Buddha.

Hardy and active.

They were fond of manly sport such as hunting. The Aṅguttara Nikāya narrates how a large number of Licchavi youths, armed with bows, ready with strings, set and surrounded by a pack of hounds, were roving about in the Mahāvana but finding the Buddha seated at the foot of a tree in the

Hunting

1. *Saṁyutta Nikāya* (P. T. S.), pt. II, 267-268.

forest, threw away their bows and arrows and sending away the pack of hounds sat by the Great Teacher, subdued by his presence, silent and without a word, in a reverent attitude with the palms joined. A Licchavi of apparently advanced years, Mahānāma by name, who came to pay his respects to the Buddha, expressed his great wonder at the sight of the Licchavi youths, full of life and vivacity, notorious for their insolent and wanton conduct in the city, thus sitting silent and demure, in an attitude of reverence before the great teacher; he pointed out the defects in their character, the defects that are found in youngmen of every country where the people are rich and powerful and of a high temperament. "The Licchavi youths, Oh Lord!" goes on Mahānāma, "are rude and rough and whatever presents are sent to the families, sugarcane or plums, cakes, sweetmeats or preparations of sugar, these they plunder and eat up, throw dust at the ladies of respectable families and girls of good families; such youngmen are now all silent and demure, are doing obeisance with joined palms to yourself, O Lord."[1] Here we get an insight into the daily life of these young cockneys glorying within the walls of the city of Vaiśālī. It shows that the young Vaiśālians, though

Influence of the Buddha on the Licchavi youths.

1. *Aṅguttara Nikāya*, P. T. S. pt. III, p. 76.

they indulged in the pranks and peccadillos of youth, were not so wild as to lose all sense of reverence or respect due to religious men.

Watters' view.

"In the Buddha's time, the young Licchavis of the city," says Watters, "were a free, wild, set, very handsome and full of life and Buddha compared them to the gods in Indra's Heaven. They dressed well, were good archers, and drove fast carriages, but they were wanton, insolent and utterly irreligious."[1]

Its criticism.

This is an exaggeration and is probably based on the Chinese translations of such passages as the following from the Lalitavistara, where some of the Tuṣita gods were pointing out the defects in the character of the Vaiśālians when their city was recommended by others among them as a suitable place of birth for the Bodhisattva. These Devaputras in the Tuṣita heaven averred, "Vaiśālī is unfit. What is the reason ? Look here. They do not speak with propriety towards each other, there is no practice of religion among them, nor obedience to those in high or middle position, nor to the old and the elders. Each one of them thinks, 'I am a king, and I am a king.' They do not accept the discipleship of any one, nor the religion of any one. Therefore is Vaiśālī unfit."[2] Whatever might

1. T. Watters, *On Yuan Chwang*, Vol. II, p. 79.
2. *Lalitavistara*, Ed. by E. Lefmann, Vol. I, p. 21. "*Apara āhuḥ sāpyapratirūpā......tena sāpyapratirūpā.*"

have been the opinions of these 'sons of heaven' before the birth of the Bodhisattva, they must have changed their opinions about the people of Vaiśālī, who showed such remarkable veneration towards the Enlightened One and received such marked favour from him. Do we not often read of five hundred Licchavis visiting him at the Kuṭāgāraśālā surrounding him and doing obeisance to him. The only conclusion we can draw from the above account in the Lalitavistara, is that the Licchavis were rather independent in character and would not easily accept a subordinate position to any one whether in politics or in religion or in ordinary daily life.

Theft almost unknown.

Theft was almost unknown among the Licchavis as a passage in the Vinaya Piṭaka indicates.[1]

Vaddha, a Licchavi, at the instigation of some dishonest Bhikkhus, had preferred a false charge of adultery against Dabba, a Mallian, but Vaddha afterwards made a clean breast of the whole ugly plot as soon as he saw the measure of his iniquity.[2]

Then again the statement that the Licchavis did not respect their elders or were irreligious, is in direct contradiction of what the Buddha said about them to Vassakāra, the Magadhan minister.

1. Vinaya Piṭakam, Ed. by H. Oldenberg, Vol IV., Bhikkhunī-Vibhanga Sanghādidesa, pp. 225-226.

2. Vinaya Texts, S. B. E, pt III, pp. 118-125.

"So long as they honour and esteem and revere and support the Vajjian elders, and hold it a point of duty to hearken to their words—so long as no women or girls belonging to their clans are detained among them by force or abduction—so long may the Vajjians be expected not to decline, but to prosper."[1]

Training of elephant.

The young Vajjians, of whose martial instincts and sportsmanlike character we have got evidence above, appear to have been in the habit of training elephants. Among the Psalms of the Brethren (Theragāthā), we find one composed by Vajjiputta, the son of a Licchavi rājā at Veśālī, who became known among the followers of Buddha as the Vajjian's son, and who in his early life was engaged in training elephants.[2] Besides being partial to these manly arts of war and sports, the Licchavis were great lovers of fine arts.

Lovers of fine arts.

Education.

The Licchavi youths went to distant countries for education. We read of a Licchavi named Mahāli who went to Taxilā to learn śilpa or arts and returned home after completing his education. It is said that he in his turn trained as many as five hundred Licchavis who also, when educated,

1. *Dialogues of the Buddha*, part II, p. 80.

2. *Psalms of the Brethren*, Translated by Mrs Rhys Davids, p. 106.

took up the same task and in this way education spread far and wide among the Licchavis.[1]

Artisans.

Artisans such as tailors, goldsmiths and jewellers must have been very much in requisition at the city of Vaiśālî to furnish the gay robes of seven thousand seven hundred and seven rājās or nobles, and we can very well imagine what a great strain the artisans were put to in order to devise suits of dress and ornaments to fit up the variously coloured Licchavis, the blues, the reds, the yellows, the greens and the whites.

Construction of palaces and shrines etc.

The art of building also was much developed in Vaiśālî; the magnificent palaces of the Licchavis are spoken of in the Lalitavistara.[2] They were equally enthusiastic in the building of temples, shrines, and monasteries for the Bhikkhus; and we are told that the Bhikkhus themselves superintended the construction of these buildings for the order. The Cullavagga of the Vinaya Piṭaka tells us also how on one occasion when the Enlightened One was staying at the peak-roofed-hall in the Mahāvana, "the people were zealously engaged in putting up new buildings (for the use of the order), and as zealously provided with the requisite clothes, and food, and lodging, and medicine for the sick,

1. *Fausboll, Dhammapadam* (*old edition*) p. 211.
2. *Lalitavistara, Chap.* 3 *p.* 23. (*Bibliotheca Indica Series.*)

all such Bhikkhus as superintended their work."[1] We are further told how a poor tailor of Vaiśālī intent on building himself a house for the Saṃgha, raised the walls of such a house, but, as the Cullavagga tells us "by his want of experience the laying was out of line and the wall fell down." Then the poor tailor felt disturbed, grew angry and murmured thus :—"These Sākyaputtiya Samaṇas exhort and teach those men who provide them with the requisite clothes, food, lodging, and medicine, and superintend their buildings for them. But I am poor and no one exhorts or teaches me or helps me in my building."[2] This passage shows that some of the Bhikkhus themselves were master builders who supervised the erection of houses for the Buddhist order, just as in the mediæval times in Europe we find the monk excelling in many of the fine arts including painting, sculpture and architecture. The Licchavis of Vaiśālī had built many shrines or Caityas inside and outside their great city and we have seen from the Mahāvastu passage quoted in the last chapter, with what great liberality and magnanimity they delivered over the best among them to Buddha and the Buddhist Church. That these Caityas were beautiful and fine buildings where one

1. *Cullavagga*, VI. Translated by Drs. Rhys Davids and Oldenberg, S. B. E. XX. pp. 189-190.

2. Ibid. p. 190.

might prefer to dwell as long as one liked, even to the end of the kalpa, appears from a passage in the Dīgha Nikāya where Buddha while staying at the Cāpāla Caitya said about each of the Caityas that it was charming and then suggested to Ânanda that the Tathāgata might be inclined to live there for a kalpa[1] or the remaining part of a kalpa, meaning perhaps that in such beautiful surroundings, life would be pleasant and worth living.

Matrimonial rites.

About the marriage rites of the Licchavis, it is said in the Tibetan books that there were rules restricting the marriage of all girls born in Vaiśālī, to that city alone. They state "the people of Vaiśālī had made a law that a daughter born in the first district could marry only in the first district, not in the second or third; that one born in the middle district could marry only in the first and second; but that one born in the last district could marry in any one of the three; moreover, that no marriage was to be contracted outside Vaiśālī."[2] A passage in the Bhikkhunī Vibhaṅga Saṅghādidesa[3] indicates that a Licchavi who wanted to marry could ask the corporation or the

Restrictions.

1. *Buddhist Suttas,* S. B. E. Vol. XI. p. 58.
2. Rockhill, *Life of the Buddha*. p. 62.
3. *Bhikkhunī Vibhaṅga Saṅghādidesa* II Vinaya Piṭakaṁ Ed. by H. Oldenberg. Vol. IV, p 225.

Licchavigaṇa to select a suitable bride for him. They appear to have a high idea of female chastity; violation of chastity was a serious offence amongst them. Buddha himself says that "no women or girls belonging to their clans are detained among them by force or abduction."[1] The Petavatthu Aṭṭhakathā gives a story of a Licchavi rājā named Ambasakkhara who was enamoured of the beauty of a married woman, whose husband he engaged as an officer under him; he wanted to gain her love but was foiled in his attempts.[2]

Chastity.

The punishment for a woman who broke her marriage vow was very severe, the husband could with impunity even take away her life. But even an adulterous woman could save herself from the punishment by entering the congregation of nuns, by getting the Pabbajjā ordination, as can be seen from the Bhikkhunī-Vibhaṅga Saṅghādisesa.

Marriage Contract inviolable—its exception

A Licchavi wife committed adultery The husband warned his wife many times but she heeded not. The Licchavi informed the Licchavigaṇa that his wife had committed adultery and he was willing

An Example.

1. *Buddhist Suttas*, S B. E., Vol. XI, pp. 3 & 4.
2. *Petavatthu-Aṭṭhakathā*, Sinhalese edition, Simon Hewavitarṇe's Bequest Series., No. I, pp. 154-156.
3. *Vinaya Piṭaka* by H. Oldenberg. Vol. IV. pp. 225-226.

to kill her; he then asked the gaṇa to select a suitable wife for him. When the lady heard that she would be killed, she took her valuables, went to Sāvatthī and asked for Pabbajjā (ordination) from the titthiyas, by whom, however, she was refused: then she went to the Bhikkhunis who in a body also refused; at last she went to a Bhikkhunī who was persuaded to give ordination to her and thus she was successful. The Licchavi went to Sāvatthī and saw his wife ordained, complained to the king Pasenadī of Kośala, who asked him to show his wife. The Licchavi informed the king that she had become a Bhikkhunī. The king said that as she had become a Bhikkhunī, no punishment could be inflicted on her.

After the occurrence of this event; an agitation was set on foot among the Licchavis who reported the matter to the Buddha who told the Bhikkhunis that they should not give ordination to such a woman.[1] Thus we see that cases of adultery were tried by the Licchavigaṇa.

They used to kill animals on the 8th, 14th and 15th day of the lunar months and eat their flesh.[2]

We have already referred in Chapter I. to the various methods prevalent among the

---

1. Bhikkhunī Vibhaṅga Saṁghādidesa, Vol II, p. 225.
2. Divyāvadāna (Cowell & Neil), p. 136.

Licchavis with regard to the disposal of the dead. Besides cremation and burial, the custom of exposing the dead to be devoured by wild animals seems to have been in existence in Vaiśālī. When the Bodhisatta was at Vaiśālī, he is said to have observed a cemetery under a clump of trees and enquired about it from the Ṛṣis who explained that the corpses of men were exposed to be devoured by birds and there they used to collect and pile up the white bones of dead persons. They burnt corpses there and the bones were preserved in heaps; the corpses were hung from the trees; there were others buried there such as had been killed by their relatives fearing lest they should be born again while others were left upon the ground that they might return, if possible, to their former homes.[1] Dr. Vincent Smith says that it proves the custom that the ancient inhabitants of Vaiśālī disposed of the dead "sometimes by exposure, sometimes by cremation, and sometimes by burial."[2]

Disposal of the dead.

The Licchavis had various festivals, of which the Sabbarattivāro or Sabbaratticāro was the most important. At the Sabbarattivāro or Sabbaratticāro festival, songs were sung, trumpets, drums

Festivals.

1. Beal's Romantic Legend of the S'ākya Buddha, pp. 159-160.
2. Indian Antiquary, Vol. XXXII, pp. 233-236.

and other musical instruments were used.[1] When a festival took place at Veśālī, all the people used to enjoy it and there were dancing, singing and recitation.[2]

Changes in Licchavi character.

It was Sāriputta who said regarding the Vajjians that they were once good and afterwards took to evil ways. In other words, at first they were free from desires of senses, ill-will, torpor, sloth, etc., but afterwards they were addicted to these evils. Then again they gave up all these vices and became good.[3]

---

1. Saṁyutta Nikāya, Vol. I., pp 201-202.
2. Psalms of the Brethren, p. 63.
3. Ibid, p. 348.

CHAPTER IV.

Religion and Philosophy.

The ideas current among the Licchavis with regard to religion and philosophy appear to have been the same as those generally prevalent in north-eastern India at the time Mahāvîra and Gautama preached their new creeds. All the information that we can get about the religion of this people is derived from Buddhist books and to a smaller extent also from Jaina works. It is apparent from what we learn about them from these sources that the Licchavis, a vigorous, manly and heroic race and highly prosperous too, were at the same time of a strongly religious and worshipful bent of mind. Both Jainism and Buddhism found many followers among them.

Introduction.

Pre-Buddhistic Religion of the Licchavis.

Even before the advent of the two new forms of religion, the Licchavis, or to call them by their wider designation, the Vajjians, appear to have been imbued with a strong religious spirit and deep devotion. The Vajjis appear to have numerous shrines in their town as well as in the country and they worshipped the deities at these shrines with proper offerings and with the observance of due rites and ceremonies. Even after Jainism and Buddhism had obtained a strong hold on the Licchavis of Vaiśālī, the great body of the people of the Vajji country as well as of the capital remained staunch followers of their ancient Brahmanic faith although they had due respect for the Arahants or Buddhist sages that wandered over their country preaching the message delivered by the Enlightened One. The Mahāparinibbāṇa Suttanta, one of the earliest composed of the Buddhist works, tells us what the Buddha told the prime minister of Magadha, Vassakāra, when he was sent by Ajātaśatru to learn from the Exalted One what he would predict with regard to his daring plan of exterminating the Vajji. The Exalted One said: "So long as the Vajjians honour and esteem and revere and support the Vajjian shrines in town or country, and allow not the proper offerings and rites, as formerly given and performed, to fall into desuetude—so long as the rightful protection, defence and support shall be fully provided for the Arahants among them, so that the Arahants from a distance may enter the realm, and the Arahants therein may live at ease—so long may the Vajjians be expected not to decline but to prosper."[1] This was said by the Buddha on the eve of his last departure for Vaiśālī and shortly before he passed away from this world.

1. T. W. and C. A F. Rhys Davids—*Dialogues of the Buddha* pt. II, p 80.

Towards the end of his life, the Licchavis were devoted worshippers at the numerous shrines that were scattered about in their country. Buddhaghosa in his commentary, the *Sumaṅgala-vilāsinī*, also observes that the Licchavis observed their old religious rites.[1] We must here bear in mind the fact that Buddhism at the early stage, of which we are speaking, was a form of faith for ascetics only, not a religious creed for all people. The Buddhists at this period only formed one of the numerous ascetic sects of Northern India. Thus there was nothing unusual in the fact that many of the Licchavis who were householders and had not accepted the life of Bhikkhus or Buddhist monks, should remain firm followers of their former faith.

From the meagre mention of the shrines of the Licchavis in the Buddhist books, it is not easy to determine what deities were worshipped in these shrines. There is, however, nothing to show that the religious belief of the Licchavis was in any way different from that of the Brāhmanic form of faith as it then obtained throughout Northern India. The Vedic religion was still in full vigour in north-eastern India, as the references, though not very numerous, to Vedic sacrifices in the Buddhist books show. We should bear in mind that the country of the Vajjis was the sacred

1. Sumaṅgalavilāsinī (Burmese Edition) pp. 103-105.

land of Mithilā where the Great Samrāt Janaka, had exercised his sway and where Yājñavalkya preached the white Yajurveda; at the same time we must not forget that there are strong reasons to suspect, as Dr. Kern observes, "that original Buddhism was not exactly that of the canonical book."[1] The Pāli Tripiṭaka represents the version acknowledged by a particular sect of the Buddhist, namely, the Vibhajjavādins of Ceylon and there can be no doubt that the sacred canon was moulded and modified by them when it was finally edited, and, as it is said, was put down in writing in Ceylon. We cannot, therefore, expect to find an impartial account of the religious tenets of the people of the country where the Enlightened Master preached his new message. But as the Buddhist along with the Jaina books form the only source of our information about the religious beliefs of the Licchavis, we have to take them as the basis of our account of their ideas of religion.

We have already referred to the numerous Caityas in Vaiśalī and its suburbs as mentioned in the Mahāvastu. These Caityas are called the Cāpāla, the Saptāmraka, the Bahuputra, the Gautama, the Kapinahya and the Markaṭahrada-tīra. In the Mahāparinibbāṇa Suttanta, we also get the names of these shrines.

1. Kern, *Manual of Indian Buddhism*, p. 50.

The Exalted One on his last visit to Vaiśālī went one day to the Cāpāla Caitya and said addressing the Venerable Ânānda : "How delightful a spot, Ânanda, is Vaiśālī, and how charming the Udena Shrine, and the Gotamaka Shrine, and the Shrine of the Seven Mangoes (Sattambaka), and the Shrine of many sons, and the Sārandada Shrine, and the Cāpāla Shrine." The Pāṭika Suttanta which like the Mahāparinibbāṇa Suttanta, is included in the Dīgha-Nikāya indicates the position of these Caityas. Kandara-masuka, a naked ascetic of Vaiśālī sought to please the Licchavis by professing a great attachment to their city ; he says, "so long as I live, I will never go beyond the Udena Shrine on the east of Vaiśālī ; the Gotamaka Shrine on the south ; the Sattamba Shrine on the west and the Bahuputta Shrine on the north."[1] From this boasting of Kandara-masuka, it is evident that these shrines were situated in the outskirts of Vaiśālī marking its boundaries, as it were. A passage in the Divyāvadāna also gives a list of the Caityas in almost the same words as the Mahāparinibbāṇa Suttanta : there also the Enlightened One speaks, addressing Ânanda, of the beauties of the Caityas called Cāpāla, Saptāmraka, Bahupattraka and Gautama-nyagrodha.[2] *Bahupattraka* is evidently

1. *Dialogues of the Buddha*, part III, p. 14.
2. *Divyāvadāna*, p. 201.

the same as *Bahuputtraka* of the other texts. Altogether we get the names of eight caityas or shrines in and about Vaiśālī. There can, therefore, be no doubt with regard to the existence of these caityas in the country of the Licchavis. Buddhaghosa in his commentary on the Mahāparinibbāṇa Suttanta explains *cetiyāni* in the text as *Yakkha-Cetiyāni* and about the Sārandada Caitya where the Buddha preached, he says that "this was a Vihāra erected on the site of a former shrine of the Yakkha Sārandada."[1] So that from Buddhaghosa's comments it is but reasonable to assume that the Yakkhas were worshipped in some of the caityas, but the materials at our command do not justify us to assume that the Yakkhas were the only deities worshipped at these shrines. The Buddhist books show that the Vedic gods, Indra and Prajāpatī or Brahmā [2] were very popular deities in the regions where the Buddha preached. The Arthaśāstra of Kauṭilya [3] also speaks of many gods popularly worshipped besides the Vedic divinities. Some scholars are of opinion that the caityas were "Shrines of pre-Buddhistic worship" and that "they were probably trees

1. *Dialogues of the Buddha*, part II. p. 80, notes 2 and 3.

2. For Brahmā see S. N. 122 seq ; Saṁy. VI. 1. 1—3, 10, &c. M. P. S. VI. 15, etc. etc.

3. Arthaśāstra of Kauṭilya, Ed. by R. Shāma Sāstrî, 2nd edition, p. 244.

and barrows."[1] Some of the caityas, as their names suggest, might have been named after the trees which marked the spots, but it would be going too far to imagine merely from the name that these shrines consisted of trees and nothing else, as some scholars would have us believe.

Jainism.

Mahāvîra, the twenty-fourth Tîrthaṅkara of the Jains, as we have seen before, was a citizen of Vaiśālī. Even before his advent, the faith of which he was the last exponent, seems to have been prevalent in Vaiśālî and the country round, in some earlier form. It appears from the Jaina accounts that the religion as fixed and established by Pārśvanātha who is revered as the twenty-third Tîrthaṅkara, was followed by some at least of the Kṣatriya people of the north-eastern India, and especially amongst the residents of Vaiśālî. We read in the Âyārānga Sūtra, "The venerable Ascetic Mahāvîra's parents were worshippers of Pārśva and followers of the Śramaṇas. During many years, they were followers of the Śramaṇas, and for the sake of protecting the six classes of lives they observed, blamed, repented, confessed, and did penance according to their sins. On a bed of Kuśa-grass they rejected all food, and their

1. Prof. and Mrs. Rhys Davids, *Dialogues of the Buddha*, pt. II, p. 110., footnote, 2. See also Mr. R. P. Chanda's *Mediæval Sculpture in Eastern India*, Cal. Univ. Journal (Arts), Vol. III,

bodies dried up by the last mortification of the flesh, which is to end in death. Thus they died in the proper month, and leaving their bodies, were born as gods in Adbhuta Kalpa."[1] Similar accounts are given in other Jaina works also of the prevalence in the country of a faith which was afterwards developed by Mahāvîra. The Śramaṇas or wandering ascetics had been in existence ever since the time of the earlier Upaniṣads and evidently the Śramaṇas that were followed so reverently by the parents of Mahāvîra belonged to one of the numerous sects or classes amongst which the Indian ascetics appear to have been divided.

After Mahāvîra developed his doctrines and preached his faith of unbounded charity to all living beings in the Vajji land and in Magadha, the number of his followers among the Licchavis appears to have been large and some men of the highest position in Vaiśālî appear to have been among them as is seen from the Buddhist books themselves. In the Mahāvagga of the Vinaya Piṭaka we read that Sîha, the general-in-chief of the Licchavis, was a disciple of Nigaṇṭha Nātaputta who has been shown by Profs. Bühler and Jacobi to be identical with Mahāvîra of the Jaina legends. We read here

1. Jaina Sūtras, pt. I., *Âkārañga Sūtra* Translated by H. Jacobi, S. B. E. Vol. xxii, p. 194.

how general Sīha,[1] a follower of the Nigaṇṭhas, gradually felt attracted towards the Samaṇa Gotama by listening to the discussions among the Licchavis at the Santhāgāra or the Mote-hall where they used to meet, discuss and settle all matters relating to politics or religion. One day "many distinguished Licchavis were sitting together assembled in the town hall and spoke in many ways in praise of the Buddha, of the Dhamma and of the Saṃgha. At that time, Sîha, the general-in-chief (of the Licchavis), a disciple of the Nigaṇṭha sect, was sitting in that assembly. And Sîha, the general, thought: Truly he, the Blessed One, must be the Arahat Buddha, since these many distinguished Licchavis who are sitting here together assembled in the town hall, speak in so many ways in praise of the Buddha, of the Dhamma and of the Saṃgha. What if I were to go and visit him, the Arahat Buddha." Sîha next asked permission to visit Buddha from the Nigaṇṭha Nātaputta, who, however, tried to dissuade him from doing so, pointing out the defects in the doctrines preached by the former. "Why should you, Sîha, who believe in the result of actions (according to their moral merit) go to visit the Samaṇa Gotama who denies the result of actions ?

1. *Vinaya Texts* translated by T. W. Rhys Davids and H. Oldenberg., S. B. E., Vol. XVII, pp, 108 f.

For the Samaṇa Gotama, Sīha, denies the result of actions; he teaches the doctrine of non-action; and in this doctrine he trains his disciples." Sīha's enthusiasm for Buddha abated for the time but it was again roused by the discussions of the other Licchavis, so that he at last did pay a visit to Buddha who gave him a long discourse on the Buddhist doctrine. Sīha was at last converted to the Buddhist faith. That the number of the followers of Mahāvīra at Vaiśālī however was very large also appears from this story of Sīha. This general had invited Buddha and the Bhikkhus to take their meal at his house and procured meat from the market for feeding them. But the Jains spread a false report as we read in the Mahāvagga: "At that time a great number of Nigaṇṭhas (running) through Vesālī, from road to road and from cross-way to cross-way, with outstretched arms, cried: To-day Sīha, the General, has killed a great ox and has made a meal for the Samaṇa Gotama; the Samaṇa Gotama knowingly eats this meat of an animal killed for this very purpose and has thus become virtually the author of that deed (of killing the animal)."[1] This false report circulated by them only made Sīha firmer in his zeal for the new faith, but the story shows that the number of the Nigaṇṭhas at Vaiśālī was sufficiently large to defy the influence of

1. Vinaya Texts, S. B. E., Vol. xvii, p. 116.

such a great man as Sīha, and the fact that the conversion of Sīha took place at the time that Buddha paid his last visit to the city, shows that though Buddhism had made many converts among the followers of the faith preached by Mahāvīra, yet they were still numerous and powerful at the capital of the Licchavis even after the numerous sermons preached by the Buddha. This is also confirmed by the story of Saccaka, a Nirgrantha, who had the hardihood to challenge the Buddha himself to a discussion on philosophical tenets, before an assemblage of five hundred Licchavis.[1]

Buddhism.

We have an ample account of the spread of Buddhism among the Licchavis from the various works in the Buddhist sacred literature. The Enlightened One had paid at least three visits, but probably many more, to the city and from the very first he appears to have met with great success among them. We have already seen from the Mahāvastu how great was the veneration with which he was received on his first visit to Vaiśālī. The Pāli works have recorded many occasions on which the Licchavis sought the aid of Buddha for the solution of numerous problems about religion and dogma that presented any difficulty to them. These questions and answers put to and given by

---

1. The story of Saccaka is given in detail in this chapter, a few pages below.

the Buddha, though frequently of only a general character and such as would naturally arise in the mind of any Buddhist, may yet help us to get glimpses of the workings of the Licchavi mind with regard to matters of faith, and we think that the bringing together of all these Licchavi questions to the Master will well repay the trouble bestowed upon them.

Bhaddiya, a Licchavi and the Buddha.

Once when the Buddha was staying in the Kūṭāgāraśālā at Mahāvana in Vaiśālī, a Licchavi named Bhaddiya paid a visit to the Buddha and told him: "I have heard that the Samaṇa Gotama is a magician who knows the magic spells by virtue of which he attracts the followers of the faiths. The Buddha replied, "Oh Bhaddiya, when you know yourself that these dhammas are sources of suffering (Akusalā), you shun them."[1]

Two Licchavis and the Buddha.

On another occasion we find that when the Buddha was at Vaiśālī, a Licchavi named Sālho and another Licchavi named Abhaya approached the Buddha. Salho, the Licchavi, said to the Buddha, "There are some Samaṇas and Brāhmaṇas who preach that a flood may be crossed by purity of sīla and tapa (penance); what does the Exalted One say about it? The Buddha

1. *Aṅguttara Nikāya*, P. T. S. Vol. II, pp. 190-194.

replied that it was impossible for the Samaṇas and the Brāhmaṇas who were not pure in deed, whether bodily or mentally and also in speech. Just as a warrior destroys a large army, so a noble disciple destroys all the creatures of Avidyā.[1]

Licchavi minister Nandaka and the Buddha.

A Licchavi minister (Mahāmātra) Nandaka approached the place where the Blessed One was, saluted him and sat at a little distance. The Buddha explained to him the four Dhammas by which a noble disciple can obtain emancipation. Nandaka was told that it was the time to take his bath. Nandaka replied, "No use having an external bath, my faith in the Blessed One will be my internal bath."[2]

Buddha's influence on Licchavi youths.

We have already recounted how when the Blessed One was at Mahāvana, many young Licchavis who having taken well-arranged bows, surrounded by dogs used to wander about in the Mahāvana, now sat silent and demure by the Buddha, who was seated at the foot of a tree and how Mahānāma, a Licchavi of rather advanced age, expressed his surprise that these arrogant youths who were rather rowdy in their daily life, had become so mild and gentle before the Exalted One.[3] On another occasion when the Buddha

---

1. *Aṅguttara Nikāya*, P. T. S. Vol. II, pp. 200-202.
2. *Saṁyutta Nikāya*, P. T. S. Vol. V. pp. 389-390.
3. *Aṅguttara Nikāya*, Vol. III, pp. 75-78.

was at Vaiśālī, there were 500 Licchavis assembled at the *Sārandadacetiya*. There was a talk about the five kinds of rare gems, Hatthiratana, Assaratana, Maṇiratana, Itthiratana and Gahapatiratana. The Licchavis placed a man on the road with instructions to inform them when he would see the Buddha coming. He informed the Licchavis about his advent. They approached him and requested him to go to the *Sārandadacetiya*. The Buddha agreed and went to the shrine. The Licchavis informed the Buddha that a discussion had arisen among them about the five kinds of rare gems. Buddha said, "The Licchavis who indulge in kāma or desire speak of such a topic." Buddha solved the problem by speaking of five kinds of precious gems. It is difficult to get such persons as realise the Tathāgata's dhamma. It is difficult to get such persons as strictly follow the Tathāgata's Dhamma. It is also difficult to find a person who is grateful and who is an exponent of gratefulness. The appearance of Tathāgata on earth is rare. So also is the preacher of Tathāgata's Dhamma.[1]

500 Licchavis and the Buddha

The Aṅguttara Nikāya[2] speaks of a large number of Licchavis, who, when going to see the Buddha who was at Vaiśālī, resounded the

1. *Aṅguttara Nikāya.* Vol, III. pp 167-168.
2. P. T. S. vol. V, p 133.

Mahāvana with a great tumult of joy on seeing the Buddha, as they were greatly devoted to him and as they had a strong faith in him. This noise so greatly troubled the Bhikkhus that they were unable to proceed with their meditation, and the Buddha remarked, "Sound is the hindrance of meditation." The Aṅguttara-Nikāya[1] narrates how on another occasion, when the Blessed One was at Vaiśālī, he was worshipped by 500 Licchavis arrayed in various coloured garments, ornaments, and trappings. The Licchavis gave Piṅgiyāni 500 upper garments, after listening to a gāthā in praise of the Buddha sung by him. Piṅgiyāni offered the Buddha three garments. Then the Buddha spoke of the five rare gems before the Licchavis.

Jubilations of the Licchavis at the sight of the Buddha.

Añjana-Vaniya was born at Vaiśālī in the family of a rājā of the Vajjians. During his adolescence, the three-fold panic of drought, sickness and non-human foes affected the Vajjian territory. Afterwards the Exalted One put a stop to the panic and addressed a great concourse. Hearing his discourse, the prince won faith and left the world. After passing through the preliminary training, he settled in the Añjana wood at Sāketa. When the rains drew near, he got a castaway couch and built over it a hut of grass and engaged himself

Anjana-Vaniya.

1. P. T. S. Vol. III, p. 239.

in a strenuous study for one month. Then he won Arhatship.[1]

Vajjiputta or the son of the Vajjis was the son of a Licchavi rājā at Vaiśālī. He went to the Vihāra to attain salvation when the Master was preaching. Hearing him he entered the order and in due course acquired six-fold Abhiññā.[2]

Vajjiputta

Sīhā, a daughter of the sister of the Licchavi general Sīha, was born at Vaiśālī at the time of Gotama Buddha. She was called Sīhā, after her maternal uncle, Sīha. When she attained years of discretion, one day she heard the Master teaching the Norm. She became a believer and obtained the consent of her parents to enter the order. When she was attempting to gain insight, she was unable to prevent her mind from running on objects of external charm. Thus harassed for seven years, she at last made up her mind to put an end to her life. Taking a noose, she hung it round the bough of a tree and having it tied round her neck, she made her mind bend upon insight. At last she won Arhatship with a thorough grasp of "the Norm in form and in meaning."[3]

Siha.

Jentī or Jentā was born in a princely family

1. *Psalms of the Brethren*, p. 56.
2. Ibid, p. 106.
3. *Psalms of the Sisters*, Translated into English by Mrs. Rhys Davids, pp. 53-54.

of the Licchavis at Vaiśālī. She won Arhatship after hearing the Dhamma preached by the Buddha. She developed the seven sambojjhaṅgas.[1]

Jenti or Jenta

Vāsiṭṭhī was reborn in a clansman's family at Vaiśālī. Her parents gave her in marriage to a clansman's son of equal position. She had a son. When the child was able to run about, he died. She being worn and overwhelmed with grief, came to Mithilā. There she saw the Exalted One, self-controlled and self-contained. At the sight of the Buddha she got back her normal mind from the frenzy that had caught hold of her. The Master taught her the outlines of the Norm. Performing all proper duties, she acquired insight and struggling with the help of full knowledge, she soon attained Arhatship together with a thorough grasp of the Norm in form and in spirit.[2]

Vasitthi.

Ambapālī was finally re-born at Vaiśālī in the king's gardens at the foot of a mango tree. She was brought by the gardener to the city. She was known as the mango-guardian's girl. She was so very beautiful that many young princes wanted to have her. She was made a courtezan. Later on, out of reverence for the Master, She built a Vihāra in her own gardens and gave it

Ambapali

1. *Psalms of the Sisters*, pp 23-24.

2, Ibid, pp. 79-80.

over to him and the order. When she heard her own son preaching the 'Norm', she tried to acquire insight.[1]

The evanescence of her own body was noticed by her and she saw transitoriness in every phenomenon of the universe. At last she attained Arhatship.[2]

Sambhūta, reborn in a clansman's family, was converted by the Treasurer of the Norm, Ânanda, and entered the order. With his developed insight he won Arhatship. Seeing the Vajjian brethren put forth the ten theses a century after the Parinibbāṇa of the Exalted One, the Thera Sambhūta moved by righteous emotion at the proposed perversion of the Dhamma and Vinaya, gave some good advice which might be stated as follows : "A man should have a definite plan and principle. One having it will not suffer, but will get ample rewards in proper time."[3]

Sambhuta

A hundred years after the passing away of the Buddha, certain Vajjiputtaka bhikkhus, the residents of Vaiśālī, began to indulge in practices prejudicial to the interests of Buddhism. They proclaimed ten indulgences as permissible, namely : "(1) storing of salt[4] ; (2) the

1. *Psalms of the Sisters*, pp. 120-121.
2. Ibid, p. 125.
3. *Psalms of the Brethren*, p. 182.
4. *Note*—Priests can keep salt only for seven days. But if kept in horn, they would be able to retain it for any length of time.—J. A. S. B. Vol. VI., pt. II.. p. 728, (1837).

taking of the midday meal when the sun's shadow shows two finger-breadths afternoon ; (3) the going to some village (or to another village) and there eating fresh food ; (4) residing (in the same parish and yet holding the Uposatha separately) ; (5) sanction (of a solemn act in an incomplete chapter) ; (6) the (unconditional) following of a precedent ; (7) the partaking of unchurned milk ; (8) of (unfermented) toddy ; (9) the use of a mat without fringes (not conform with the model prescribed) ; (10) to accept gold and silver.[1]

Ten indulgences and Vajjiputtaka bhikkhus.

At this period, the venerable Yaso, the son of Kākaṇḍaka, during his pilgrimage in the Vajji country heard of these ten indulgences being preached and practised by the Bhikkhus and thus meditated, "Having myself heard of the calamity which is impending over the religion of the deity gifted with ten powers, should I be deficient in my exertions (to avert it), that proceeding would be unbecoming of me : wherefore disgracing these impious (characters), let me glorify Dhamma." Thus meditating he went to the Kūṭāgāra Hall in the Mahāvana at Vaiśālī. The Bhikkhus of Vaiśālī, on the Uposatha day in question, filling a golden basin with water, and placing

Yaso.

1. Kern's *Manual of Buddhism*, p. 103,

it in the midst of the assembled priests, thus appealed to the devotees of Vaiśālī, who attended there, "Beloved ones ! bestow on the priesthood either a kahāpaṇa or half, or a quarter of one, or even the value of a māsa, to the priesthood, it will afford the means of providing themselves with sacerdotal requisites." Seven hundred neither more nor less were selected (for the convocation). From this circumstance this convocation on the Vinaya is also called the "Sattasatika" (the convocation of the seven hundred). At this meeting, twelve thousand Bhikkhus assembled, brought together by the exertions of the venerable Yaso. In the midst of these discussions, by the interrogation of the venerable Revata, and by the exposition of the Vinaya by the Thera Sabbakāmi, the ten indulgences being thoroughly inquired into, a judgment of suppression was finally pronounced.[1]

Judgment of suppression finally pronounced

Mr. Beal in his Romantic Legend of Śākya Buddha[2] says that the people of Vaiśālī owing to their imperfect knowledge of the laws of self-discipline and mortification, could not use true discernment in their religious life

Beal's opinion regarding the inhabitants of Vaisali

1. *Examination of the Pāli Buddhistical Annals*, Vol. VI, part II, p. 729, J. A. S. B., 1837 (September).

2. *Romantic Legend of Śākya Buddha from the Chinese Sanskrit*, pp. 167-168.

and search after deliverance. There was an old king named Druma, for example, in the city of Vaiśālī, who retired into solitude, but afterwards forsaking his hermit cell, came back to govern his kingdom with justice.

Druma, an old King of Vaisali.

But we cannot agree with Mr. Beal. It is evident from the Psalms of the Brethren and Sisters that many people of Vaiśālī, both male and female, though they had fallen off from virtue at first, were, later on, greatly influenced by the preaching of the Norm and became self-controlled and self-disciplined. They advanced so far as to attain Arhatship which they could not have gained if they had failed to use true discernment in their religious life and search after deliverance.

Beal's opinion discussed.

The influence that the teachings of the Exalted One exercised upon the fierce Licchavis, is unique. Of the many stories showing how noble and inspiring were the Blessed One's teachings, we give below one indicating how they cured a wicked prince of the ferocity of his spirit and temper.

It has been said of a wicked Licchavi prince[1] that he was so very fierce, cruel, passionate and vindictive that none could dare to utter more than

1. Ekapaṇṇa Jātaka (Cowell's Edition) Vol. I. p. 316.

two or three words in his presence, even his parents, relations and friends, could not make him better. So at last his parents resolved to bring him to the All-wise Buddha for his rectification. Accordingly he was brought before the Buddha who addressed and said to him thus—"Prince ! a man should not be cruel, passionate and ferocious because such a man is harsh and unkind to his father, mother, brother, sister, children, friends, relatives and to all and thus he is looked upon with terror and hatred by all. He will be reborn in hell or other place of punishment after this life ; and however adorned he may be in this life, he looks ugly ; although his face is beautiful like the orb of the full moon, yet it is loathsome like a scorched lotus or disc of gold overworn with filth. The violence of his rage impels him to commit suicide and thus meeting his death by reason of his own rage he is reborn into torment. So also those persons who injure others are not only hated in this life but will after their body's death, pass to hell and punishment and when they are again born as men they are destined to be beset with disease and sickness of eye and ear. So let all men show kindness and also do good to others and thereby they will avoid hell and punishment."

Wicked Licchavi prince.

The magic power of this wholesome and edifying lecture had the beneficial effect of removing the arrogance and selfishness of the prince from the core of his heart, which became afterwards full of love and kindness.

Now the influence of the Buddha's teachings which changed the mood of the wicked prince was observed by the brethren who talked together as to how a single lecture could tame the fierce spirit of the prince while the ceaseless exhortations of his parents were of no avail. They also remarked thus "as an elephant-tamer or a horse-tamer makes the animal go to the right or left so the Blessed One—the All-wise Buddha, guides the man whithersoever he wills, along any of the eight directions and makes his pupil discern shapes external to himself. The Blessed One is hailed as chief of the trainers of men, supreme in bowing men to the yoke of truth. There is no trainer of men like unto the supreme Buddha." The people of Vaiśālī were so devoted to the Buddha that they made a cairn at Vaiśālī over the remains of the Buddha and celebrated a feast.[1]

Philosophical problems.

From what has been given above about the religious problems of the Licchavis, it must have become sufficiently clear that many of them were of a religious turn of mind. We shall further show that the people of Vaiśālī were meditative and very

1. Mahāparinibbāṇa Suttanta, Buddhist Suttas (S. B. E.), Vol. XI, p. 134.

often dealt with philosophical questions relating to Nirvāṇa,[1] the means of attaining Nirvāṇa,[2] *dosa, moha, adosa, amoha,*[3] *sīla, samādhi, paññā, vimutti,*[4] and the influence of the purity of *sīla, tapa,* etc.[5]

Philosophy was much cultured and developed by them. Serious problems relating to the destruction of action, destruction of sensation,[6] etc., engaged the attention of the Licchavis. They took delight in Jhānas.[7] Dr. Barua in his *Prolegomena to a study of the History of Buddhist Philosophy* (p. 42) says that the Vijjiputtakas or Vātsiputriyas were soul theorists and their conception of soul (Âtmā) or personality was quite distinct from the Sānkhya or Vedānta conception. They believed in the existence of hell specially the Sattussadam Nirayaṃ.[8] They held that a sinner was to suffer in hell on account of his evil deeds.

Saccaka, a nigantha and the Licchavis.

When the Blessed One was at Vaiśālī, 500 Licchavis assembled in the Santhāgāra on account of some business. The Nigaṇṭha Nāthaputta Saccaka approached the place where the Licchavis were and said to the Licchavis "Let

1. *Saṁyutta Nikāya,* IV, pp. 261-262.
2. *Aṅguttara Nikāya,* pt. I, pp. 220-222.
3. *Ibid,* pt. II, pp. 190-194.
4. *Ibid,* pt II.
5. *Ibid,* pt II, pp 200-202.
6. *Ibid,* pt I. pp. 220-222.
7. *Ibid,* pt II, p. 191.
8. *Petavatthu* (P. T. S.) pp. 45-46.

the Licchavis come out to-day ; I shall hold a conversation with Samaṇa Gotama. If the Samaṇa Gotama places me in the same position in which I am placed by the monk Assajī who is a Sāvaka, I shall defeat Samaṇa Gotama by my argument like a strong man catching hold of a goat by its long hair and moving it in any way he likes." Saccaka mentioned various ways in which he was going to treat Samaṇa Gotama, if Samaṇa Gotama would be defeated. Some Licchavis enquired how Gotama would meet the argument of Saccaka, the Nigaṇṭhaputta, and *vice versa*, while others enquired how Nigaṇṭhaputta Saccaka would meet the arguments of Samaṇa Gotama and *vice versa*. Saccaka induced 500 Licchavis to go with him to the Mahāvana to listen to his discussion with Gotama. He approached the place where the Bhikkhus were walking up and down and asked them, "we are anxious to see Gotama, the Blessed One." The Buddha was seated to spend the day in meditation at the foot of a tree in the Mahāvana forest. Nigaṇṭhaputta Saccaka with a large number of Licchavis went to the Blessed One and having exchanged friendly greetings with him, sat at a little distance. Some Licchavis saluting him took their seats ; others exchanged friendly greetings with him and then took their seats ; some saluting with folded hands, sat at a little distance ; some prominent Licchavis giving out their names and family names, took their seats at a little distance. Some remained silent and sat at a little distance with great devotion to the Blessed One. Then arguments relating to the saṃghas and gaṅas, some knotty points of Buddhist psychology and some knotty metaphysical questions, were started between Nigṇṭhaputta Saccaka and the Blessed One. Saccaka being defeated, invited the Blessed One who accepted the invitation. The Licchavis were informed of this and asked to bring whatever they liked at the dinner which would be held on the following day. At the break of day, the Licchavis brought five hundred dishes for the Buddha.[1] The Nigaṇṭhaputta and the Licchavis became greatly devoted to the Blessed One.

Mahali, a Licchavi.

Then again we read of Mahāli, a Licchavi, who went to the Buddha and told him that Pūraṇa Kassapa was of opinion that there was no cause of the sin of beings and without cause they suffered and there was no cause of the purity of being and without cause they were purified. Buddha refuted this theory of Pūraṇa Kassapa by raising the subtle philosophical discussion about the five khandas and afterwards the Buddha succeeded in making him understand that what Pūraṇa Kassapa had taught him did not hold good: it fell to the ground

[1] [illegible]

The Saṃyutta Nikāya relates that when the Blessed One was at Ukkācelā in the Vajji country with a large congregation of monks, he was told that owing to the passing away of Sāriputta and Moggallāna, the congregation seemed to be empty. Buddha said, "You depend on yourself and not on others. Meditate on four satipaṭṭhānas. Tathāgata has no grief or lamentation for the passing away of such great disciples because what is born for some cause is subject to decay."[1]

Buddha on sin and merit.

The Aṅguttara Nikāya[2] also speaks of a Licchavi named Mahāli who said to the Buddha, "What is the cause of sinful act?" The Blessed One answered, "If a person's mind is bent upon evil thoughts, avarice, hatred, delusion, surely he accumulates sins. If a person be free from these, he accumulates merits."

Abhaya, a Licchavi.

When Ânanda was at Vaiśālī, Abhaya, a Licchavi and another Licchavi named Paṇḍitakumāra went to Ânanda. Abhaya said to Ânanda, "Nigaṇṭha Nātha putta is all-knowing, all-seeing, knows the light of knowledge (i. e. has insight into knowledge); he comes to know by meditation the destruction of old actions. From the destruction of action there is the cessation of suffering;

1. Vol. V. pp. 163-165.
2. Vol. N. pp. 86-87.

from the cessation of suffering, we have the destruction of sensation and for the destruction of sensation, suffering will be no longer on earth. There is an overcoming of suffering by purity in the present existence." The three kinds of purity which are not subject to decay have been expounded by the Buddha. These three kinds of purity are the means of attaining Nirvāṇa and overcoming suffering.[1]

Samandaka and Sariputta.

The Saṃyutta Nikāya[2] relates that when Sāriputta dwelt at Ukkācelā among the Vajjians, a monk named Sāmaṇḍaka went to the place where Sāriputta was and asked him, "What is Nirvāṇa?" "It means *rāgakkhaya*, *dosakkhaya* and *mohakkhaya*; there is a path for the realisation of Nirvāṇa." "What is that path?" "It is the sublime eightfold path e.g. right speech, right action, etc."

Uggo, a Licchavi house-holder.

In the same Nikāya[3] we find that when the Blessed One was dwelling at Vaiśālī, Uggo, a Licchavi householder of Vaiśālī approached him and asked him thus, "why do some obtain Parinibbāṇa in the present existence while others do not?" It was replied that he who was free from attachment obtained Parinibbāṇa

1. Aṅguttara Nikāya, Vol. I. (P. T. S.) pp. 220-221.
2. Saṃyutta Nikāya, Vol. IV. (P. T. S.), pp. 261-262.
3. Ibid p. 109.

in this existence and he who was not free from attachment did not.

It is stated in the Aṅguttara Nikāya[1] that lobha, dosa or moha arises in a man internally for bad. It does not at all arise for good. A garrulous man only for avarice kills men, steals and speaks falsehood. Buddha explains dosa, lobha and moha and he distinctly states that these are for man's adversity and he further states "Alobha, adosa and amoha arise for the good of the people. A good man teaches his disciples to remove his lobha, dosa and moha." This was preached by the Buddha to Bhaddiya, a Licchavi, who was delighted and Bhaddiya requested Buddha to have him as his Sāvaka. The Buddha accepted him as his disciple and said, "If I be successful in inducing all rich khattriyas and brāhmins to give up all *akusalas* and perform *kusalas*, it will be good." The same Nikāya[2] relates that Uggo, an officer of the Licchavis, had extraordinary qualities. As soon as he saw the Buddha, strong faith arose in him and he became one of his devoted followers.

Bhaddiya, a Licchavi.

Uggo, a Licchavi Officer.

1. Aṅguttara Nikāya, (P. T. S.), part. II. pp. 190-194.
2. Ibid., IV., p. 212.

CHAPTER V.

Government and Administration of Justice.

The Licchavis formed a great and powerful republic; there was no hereditary sovereign, the power of the state being vested in the assembly of citizens, each of whom called himself a rājā or king. This form of government as described in the Buddhist books was not rare in ancient India; there is ample evidence to show that in ancient times this form was much more in vogue than we are led to imagine from later literature. It is certainly a very remarkable phenomenon that while to the south of the Ganges, in Magadha, an empire was being built up first under the Śiśunākas, next under the Nandas and later still under the Mauryas, to the north of the same river, the Licchavis formed a powerful republic which defied for long the might of the Magadhan monarchs; yet we must remember that imperialism, as such, was a later product in India; in fact, we do not come across any such thing before Candra Gupta Maurya.

Republic—no hereditary ruler.

The Licchavis formed what is called in

N

ancient Indian literature, a *Samgha* or *Gaṇa*, that is, an organised corporation. One of the Buddhist canonical books, the Majjhima Nikāya,[1] speaks of the Vajjis and the Mallas as forming saṃghas and gaṇas, that is, clans governed by an organised corporation and not by an individual sovereign, the power of the state being vested in the corporation. The Mahāvastu[2] says that when plague raged in their city, one of them, Tomara, was elected by the Gaṇa to represent their difficulties before the Buddha and bring him over to their city.

The Licchavi Samgha and Gana.

Kautilya on Licchavi Samgha.

Kauṭilya, the great minister of the first Maurya Emperor, has also indicated in his Arthaśāstra the real nature of the Licchavi form of government. He speaks of the Licchavis in the chapter on the conduct of corporations.[3] He says that the saṃghas or corporations of the following people, viz, the Licchavis, the Vṛjis, the Mallas, the Madras, the Kukuras, the Kurus, the Pāñcālas and others "lived by the title of a rājā"; this apparently means that among these peoples, each one called himself a Rājā, that is, an independent ruler who did not owe allegiance or pay revenue to any one else; but each of them

1. P. T. S. Vol. I, p. 231.
2. Vol. I, p. 254.
3. Arthaśāstra translated by R. Shamasastry p. 455.

held up his head high and not merely looked upon himself as a rājā but to him the word 'rājā' had come to be a usual designation which was recognised not only by his fellow clansmen but also by the other peoples of India. Kautilya's characterisation of such people "as living by the title of a rājā"—*Rājaśabdopajivinah*—does clearly indicate that each one of them individually did not exercise the function of a rājā or sovereign ; the real power and authority of the rājā or sovereign must have been vested in the saṃgha or corporation while each of them individually had only the title Rājā. This is corroborated by the description given of the Licchavis in the Lalita·Vistara which though a comparatively later work yet evidently preserves the tradition in a correct form when it says that at Vaiśālī there was no respect for age, nor for position, whether high or middle or low ; each one there thought "I am a king and I am a king."[1] Even the lowest there did not think themselves in any way inferior to others who happened to enjoy a higher position by reason of rank or wealth. Similarly the Mahāvastu[2] speaks of the twice eighty four thousand Licchavi rājās residing within the city of Vaiśālī, thus showing that all the Licchavis living

1. Ed. Lefmann, Vol. I., p. 21.
2. Vol. I, p. 271.

in Vaiśālī were rājās. The Pāli commentaries, as for example, the preambles to the Cullakāliṅga Jātaka[1] and the Ekapaṇṇa Jātaka[2] speak of 7707 rājās of Vaiśālī. Throughout the Pāli literature also we find numerous passages in which an individual Licchavi is called a rājā as will be apparent from the numerous passages that we have quoted from the Buddhist literature in previous chapters. Kauṭilya's account shows that this designation of each individual clansman was not confined to the Licchavis alone but was shared by them along with many other warrior peoples of northern India from the land of the Madras on the north-western frontier up to the Vṛji land in the east; we happen to possess independent corroborative evidence of this statement of Kauṭilya's in the Buddhist literature with regard to the Licchavis. The same state of things must have been in existence among the other tribes mentioned by Kauṭilya.

Kauṭilya[3] observes about all these saṃghas that by virtue of their being united in such corporations, they were unconquerable by others; this shrewd politician[4] further observes that for

1. Fausboll, Vol. III., p. 1.
2. Fausboll, Vol. I., p. 504.
3. Saṁghābhisaṁhatatvāt dhriṣyān pareṣāṁ.—Arthaśāstra (2nd Ed) p. 378.
4. Saṁgha lābho daṇḍa mitralābhānāmuttamaḥ—Ibid., p. 378.

a king, the winning over to his side of such a corporate body was the acquisition of a best friend, that of all his allies, a corporation was the best and most helpful because of the power derived from their union which made them invincible. Buddhist books testify that the Licchavis were so strong as to defy the aggression of their country by any foreign power on account of their unity and concord and their practice of constantly meeting in their popular assemblies, and that this made them almost invincible. When Ajātaśatru sent his prime minister to ascertain the views of the Buddha with regard to his proposed extermination of the Vṛjis, the Blessed one said addressing Ânanda, "Have you heard, Ânanda, that the Vajjians hold full and frequent public assemblies ?" "Lord, so I have heard," replied he, " So long, Ânaṇda," rejoined the Blessed one, "as the Vajjians hold these full and frequent public assemblies ; so long may they be expected not to decline but to prosper."[1] And in like manner questioning Ânanda and receiving a similar reply, the Exalted one declared the other conditions which would ensure the welfare of the Vajjian confederacy :—"So long, Ânaṇda, as the Vajjians meet together in concord and rise in concord and carry out their undertakings in concord—so

Unity of the Licchavis.

1. Buddhist Suttas, S. B. E, Vol. IX, p. 3.

long as they enact nothing not already established, abrogate nothing that has been already enacted, and act in accordance with the ancient institutions of the Vajjians as established in former days—so long as they honour and esteem and revere and support the Vajjian elders and hold it a point of duty to hearken to their words—so long may the Vajjians be expected not to decline but to prosper."[1] From the above statements about the Licchavis we come to learn that they were governed by an assembly where the people of their clan met for discussion about all matters and we see further that these meetings were held often and frequently. The public hall where they used to hold these meetings was called the Santhāgāra and there they discussed both religion and politics. We have seen in the story of the conversion of Sīha that the Licchavis met at the Santhāgāra to discuss the teaching of the Buddha. The procedure that was followed in these assemblies in arriving at a decision on any particular matter before the council of the Licchavi saṃgha, may be gathered, as Professor D. R. Bhāndārkar[2] has pointed out, from an account of the procedure followed at the ceremony of ordination at the saṃgha of the Buddhist

Santhagara—public hall.

Procedure of the Assembly.

1. Buddhist Suttas, S. B. E., Vol. XI, pp. 3 & 4.
2. Carmichael Lectures, 1918., p. 181.

Bhikkhus. There can be no doubt that in organising the Buddhist saṃgha, the Buddha had, as his model, the political saṃghas of north-eastern India, especially that of the Licchavis whose corporation, as we have seen above from the discourse of the Buddha with Vassakāra, the Magadhan minister—he esteemed very highly. And we further observe from the Mahāparinibbāṇa Suttanta[1] that just after speaking of the great merits of the Licchavi institutions, the Exalted one called together in the service-hall at Rājagṛha all the members of the Buddhist congregation in the neighbourhood of that city and impressed on them that the virtues that he had extolled in the Licchavis were indispensable for the welfare of every organised community. Fortunately for us, the rules of procedure followed in the Buddhist community or saṃgha have been preserved in the description of the *Upaṣampadā* or ordination ceremony in the Pātimokha section of the Vinaya Piṭaka, and from it we can form an idea of the procedure followed in the political saṃgha of the Licchavis. First of all, it appears, was elected an officer called the *Āsana-Paññāpaka* or regulator of seats whose function seems to have been to seat the members of the congregation in the order of their seniority.[2] As in the Buddhist congregation,

1. *Buddhist Suttas*, pp. 5—11. (S. B. E. Vol. XI.)
2. *Vinaya Texts*, S. B. E., Vol. XX, p. 408. F.

so among the Licchavis, the elders of the clans were highly respected as we see from the Mahāparinibbāṇa Suttanta of the Dīgha Nikāya.[1]

We next come to the form of moving a resolution in the council thus assembled and seated by the *Āsana-Paññāpaka*. "The mover first announces to the assembled Bhikkhus what resolution he is going to propose : this announcement is called *Natti*. After the Ñatti, follows the question put to the Bhikkhus present if they approve the resolution. This question is put either once or three times ; in the first case we have a *Nattidutiya Kamma* ; in the second case, a *Nattikatuttha Kamma*."[2] This last process in which the question is put three times after the *Natti* or *Jñāpti* is illustrated by the process prescribed by the Buddha for the Upasampadā ordination given in the Mahāvagga. "I prescribe, O Bhikkhus, that you confer the *Upasampadā* ordination by a formal act of the order in which the announcement (ñatti) is followed by three questions.

'And you ought, O Bhikkhus, to confer the *Upasampadā* ordination in this way : Let a learned, competent Bhikkhu proclaim the following ñatti before the saṃgha :

'Let the Saṃgha, reverend Sirs, hear me.

1. *Buddhist Suttas*, S. B. E. Vol. XI, p, 3.
2. Rhys Davids & Oldenberg—*Vinaya Texts*, pt. I, p. 19, Note 2.

This person N. N. desires to receive the *Upasampadā* ordination from the venerable N. N. (i. e. with the venerable N. N. as his Upajjhāya or Upādhyāya). If the Saṃgha is ready, let the Saṃgha confer on N. N. the *Upasampadā* ordination with N. N. as Upajjhāya. This is the ñatti.

'Let the Saṃgha, reverend Sirs, hear me. This person N. N. desires to receive the *Upasampadā* ordination from the venerable N. N. The Saṃgha confers on N. N. the *Upasampadā* ordination with N. N. as Upajjhāya. Let any one of the venerable brethren who is in favour of the *Upasampadā* ordination of N. N. with N. N. as Upajjhāya, be silent, and any one who is not in favour of it, speak.

'And for the second time I thus speak to you : Let the Saṃgha (&c., as before).

'And for the third time I thus speak to you : Let the Saṃgha...&c.

'N. N. has received the *Upasampadā* ordination from the saṃgha with N. N. as Upajjhāya. The Saṃgha is in favour of it, therefore it is silent. Thus I understand.'"[1]

Disputes settled by votes.

As might be expected in such a democratic assembly, there were often violent disputes and quarrels with regard to controversial topics. In such cases the disputes were settled by the votes of the majority and this voting was by ballot ;

1. Rhys Davids and Oldenberg—*Vinaya Texts*, Pt. I, pp. 169-170.

voting tickets or salākas were served out to the voters and an officer of approved honesty and impartiality was elected to collect these tickets or voting papers. This is evidenced by the Cullavagga which recounts it thus : "Now at that time the Bhikkhus in chapter (Saṃgha) assembled, since they became violent, quarrelsome and disputatious, and kept on wounding one another with sharp words, were unable to settle the disputed question (that was brought before them). They told this matter to the Blessed one."

"I allow you, O Bhikkhus, to settle such a dispute by the vote of the majority. A Bhikkhu who shall be possessed of five qualifications shall be appointed as taker of voting tickets—one who does not walk in partiality, one who does not walk in malice, one who does not walk in folly, one who does not walk in fear, one who knows what (votes) have been taken and what have not been taken." The appointment of this officer who was called the Salākā-gāhāpaka was also made by the whole assembly.[1]

Absentee's vote counted

There was also a provision for taking votes of the members who could not for any reason be present at a meeting of the assembly. The Mahāvagga mentions an example. On an occasion when the Buddha asked all the Bhikkhus

1. Cullavagga, S. B E. Vol. XX., Vinaya texts, pt. III. p. 25.

to assemble in the saṃgha, "a certain Bhikkhu said to the Blessed One: 'There is a sick Bhikkhu, Lord, who is not present.' I prescribe, O Bhikkhus, that a sick Bhikkhu is to declare (lit. to give) his consent (to the act to be performed) etc."[1] This declaration of consent of an absent member to an official act was called *Chanda* (*Khanda*).

Quorum

A quorum was required and difficulty was often experienced in getting the right number, so that the Buddha exhorted the Bhikkhus to help to complete the quorum.[2] There are other detailed rules in the Vinaya Piṭaka for the regulation of the assembly. This elaboration and perfection of the procedure as well as the use of so many technical names to designate each particular detail shows that the organisation of these democratic assemblies had already been developed and elaborated among the political saṃghas like that of the Licchavis and that the Buddha only adopted them for the regulation of his religious saṃgha or congregation.[3]

Nayaka-chief magistrate

The Tibetan works mention a Nāyaka who was the chief magistrate of the Licchavis and was elected by the people or

1. Mahāvagga, S. B. E., XIII, p. 277.
2. Ibid, pp. 307-309.
3. For the democratic organisation of the Licchavis, see Prof. D. R. Bhāndārkar's *Carmichael Lectures* 1918, pp. 179-184.

"rather by the ruling clans of the Licchavis."[1] We do not know exactly what his functions were; perhaps he was an executive officer for carrying out the decisions of the assembly. There does not appear to have been any chief of the position of Suddhodana among the Śākyas. The preamble to the Ekapaṇṇa Jātaka[2] relates that, of the rājās who lived in Vaiśālī permanently exercising the rights of sovereignty, there were 7707 and there were quite as many Uparājas or subordinate officials, quite as many Senāpatis or generals and quite as many Bhāṇḍāgārikas or treasurers. A passage in the preamble to the Cullakāliṅga Jātaka[3] also says, "of the Licchavi Rājās, 7707 Licchavis had their abodes at Vaiśālī. All of them were given to arguments and disputations." Now what are these Licchavi Rājās mentioned in the preambles to the two Jātakas? It will be observed that for the phrase "7707 Rājās" in the first passage above referred to, there is substituted "7707 Licchavis" in the second. We may therefore take it that the two terms Rājā and Licchavi are synonymous. The form in which the sentences are put, shows that the Rājūs and the Rājās are not identical. The word Rājūka occurs in the inscriptions of

Rajas, Uparajas and Bhandagarikas.

1. Rockhill, *Life of the Buddha*, p. 62.
2. Fausboll, Vol. I, p. 504.
3. Ibid, Vol. III, p. 1,

Asoka[1] in the sense of a high official and we know that Rājā and Rājūka mean the same thing, the suffix 'ka' at the end being added without signifying any change in the meaning. Therefore it is evident that the word Rāju is used here in the sense of a high official. We take it that Rājūs were the representatives of the Licchavi Rājās at the general assembly in which was vested the right of exercising the sovereign authority. The number 7707 cannot be the number of all the Licchavis living in the town of Vaiśālī; it would be too small a number for a great people that commanded respect for many centuries for their prowess and power and also it is too small a number for a people that filled almost the whole of such a large city as Vaiśālī; in fact, we are told by the Mahāvastu that the Licchavis who went out of their capital, Vaiśālī, to meet the Buddha on his first visit to their city, numbered so many as twice 84 thousand which was not an incredible number for such an extensive city as Vaiśālī which itself denotes, as we have said before, 'the large city' by preference. We, however, do not insist upon 7707 representing the exact number of members of the ruling assembly; it is evidently an artificially concocted number, seven being used from the idea that it has some magic potency; 7707

---

1. "Sarvata vijite mama Yutā ca Rājūke ca Prādesike ca"—Rock Edict. III, Girnār Version.

means simply a large number. It is significant that none of the canonical texts themselves give this number, which occurs only in a later commentary, the Nidānakathā of the Jātakas. We do not agree with Prof. Bhāndārkar when he says that an Uparājā, a Senāpati or general and a treasurer formed the private staff of every Licchavi rājā. It simply means that the state had a large number of these officers. If stress is laid upon the fact that all these officers are said to be equal in number with the rājās or high officials, it would mean that each of the representatives had a personal staff of these three officers who helped him in discharging his duties to the state. But there is nothing to show in the texts that a group of these three officers was attached to each of the 7707 members. The whole of the statement simply signifies that the number of Licchavi representatives as well as of the officers was very large. There is, moreover, nothing to show that each of these Licchavis had, as Professor Bhāndārkar thinks, a personal property of his own which was managed by himself with the help of the three officers mentioned above. On the other hand, it is more likely that the land was held as the property of the whole state, that is, as the common property of all the Licchavi residents of Vaiśālī, each resident having only the śabda or title, rājā.

There must have been officers who recorded

the decisions of the council. A passage in the Mahā Govinda Suttanta of the Dīgha Nikāya seems to justify this conclusion. In describing a meeting of the thirty three gods in the Tāvatiṃsa heaven, it is said that after the deliberations were over, four great kings recorded the conclusions arrived at. We read in the Suttanta, "Then the three-and-thirty gods having thus deliberated and taken counsel together concerning the matter for which they were assembled and seated in the Hall of Good Counsel, with respect to that matter the Four Kings were receivers of the spoken word, the Four Great Kings were receivers of the admonition given, remaining the while in their places not retiring." On this passage the translators observe, "This sounds very much as if the Four Great Kings were looked upon as Recorders (in their memory, of course) of what had been said. They kept the minutes of the meeting. If so (the gods being made in the image of men) there must have been such Recorders at the meetings in the Mote Halls of the clans."[1] This remark is quite justified and without such officers to record the proceedings of such a vast assembly as that of the Licchavis, any practical work would have been impossible.

Records of the decisions of the council.

1. Dialogues of the Buddha, pt. II, pp. 263-264.

A passage in the preamble to the Bhaddasāla Jātaka mentions a tank, the water of which was used at the ceremony of *Abhiṣeka* or coronation of the *Kulas* or families of the gaṇa-rājās of Vaiśālī.[1] This coronation may refer to the ceremony performed when a Licchavi rājā was elected to a seat in the assembly of the state, or it may denote that the ceremony of coronation was performed when a young Licchavi kumāra or prince as he was called, succeeded to the title and position of his father.

Coronation ceremony.

The Aṭṭhakathā or commentary of Buddhaghosa on the Mahāparinibbāṇa Suttanta gives an account of the judicial procedure. When a person was presented before the Vajjian rājās as having committed an offence, they without taking him to be a malefactor, surrendered him to the *Viniccaya-Mahāmāttas* or *Viniścaya-mahāmātras*, that is, officers whose business it was to make enquiries and examine the accused with a view to ascertain whether he was guilty or innocent. If they found that the man was not a culprit, they released him, but if, on the other hand, they considered him guilty, then instead of proceeding to inflict punishment upon him, they made him over to the *Vohārikas* or *Vyavahārikas*, that

Administration of Criminal Justice.

1. Fausboll, Jātaka, Vol. IV, p. 144. See also Prof. D. R. Bhāndārkar's Carmichael Lectures, 1918, pp. 150-151.

is, persons learned in law and custom. They could discharge him if they found him innocent; if they held him guilty, then they transferred him to certain officers called *Suttadharas*, that is, officials who kept up the sūtra or the thread of law and custom existing from the ancient times. They in their turn made further investigation and if satisfied that the accused was innocent, they discharged him. If, however, he was considered guilty by them, then he was made over to the *Aṭṭhakūlakā*[1] (lit. "the eight castes or tribes") which was evidently a judicial institution composed of judges representing eight kulas or tribes.

The *Aṭṭhakūlakā*, if satisfied of the guilt of the offender, made him over to the *Senāpati* or commander of the army who made him over to the *Uparājā* or sub-king, and the latter in his turn, handed him over to the *Rājā*. The *Rājā* released the accused if he was innocent; if he was found guilty, the *Rājā* referred to the Paveṇipotthaka, that is, the Pustaka or book recording the law and precedents. This book prescribed the punishment for each particular offence. The *Rājā*, having measured the culprit's offence by means of that standard, used to inflict a proper sentence.[2]

1. Hon. G. Turnour says that no satisfactory explanation can be obtained as to the nature of the office held by these functionaries. It is inferred to be a judicial institution composed of judges from all the eight castes. (An examination of the Pāli Buddhistical Annals by G. Turnour, p. 993. f. J. A. S. B. Dec. 1838).

2. G. Turnour, An examination of the Pāli Buddhistical Annals. J. A. S. B., December 1838, pp. 993-994. ff.

CHAPTER VI.

Political History.

It is from the Buddhist literature that we first realise the importance of the Licchavis as a great and powerful kṣatriya race in north-eastern India. It is remarkable that while the Mallas, their immediate neighbours, are mentioned in the great Epic, the Mahābhārata, the Licchavis are not found among the races or peoples that were met by the Pāṇḍava brothers either in their peregrinations on pilgrimage, or on their mission of conquest at the time of the Rājasūya or the Aśvamedha. In the sixth century B. C. they came to our notice in the Jaina and Buddhist books but we meet them there as a powerful people in the enjoyment of great prosperity and of a high social status among the ruling races of eastern India, and as we have seen in the previous chapter, they had already evolved an almost perfect system of democratic government and polity embodying all the latest methods of securing independence in giving votes. It must have taken a long time to develop such an institution which can only grow in the course of many centuries. But we must not imagine that the system was a creation of the Licchavis; on the other hand, it seems that the saṃgha form of government was the normal form in ancient India even among the peoples that had a king at the head. The earliest Indian tradition of a king was that of a person elected by the people and ruling for the good of the people, as the story of Beṇa and Pṛthu in the Mahābhārata[1] clearly proves. The procedure of conducting the deliberations of an assembly must have been developing from the earliest Vedic times as the samiti and the pariṣad were well known institutions in the Ṛigveda. The Licchavis must have modelled their procedure on that which was already in vogue among the Indian Aryans and adapted it for their own use. We shall not be far mistaken if we allow a century for the evolution of the particular form of government of the Licchavis from the already existing system. Their emergence from obscurity may, therefore, fairly be placed at the beginning of the seventh century B. C. It is true that we do not find the Licchavis among the Vedic peoples but in the fourth century B. C. at the time Kauṭilya wrote, they were placed side by side with the Kurupāñcālas and Madras, some of the most powerful races in the time of the Brāhmaṇa literature of the Vedas.

We know nothing of the history of the Licchavis during the period they grew up and developed into the noble and power-

---

1. *Śāntiparva*, Ch. 60, verse 94, Vaṅgavāsī edition.

ful people as we find them in the Buddhist works. The earliest political fact of any importance that we know of is that they had given one of their daughters in marriage to Seṇiya or Śreṇika Bimbisāra, king of the gradually extending monarchy of Magadha. The Licchavi lady, according to the Nirayāvalī Sūtra, one of the early works of the Jainas, was Cellanā, the daughter of Ceṭaka, one of the rājās of Vaiśālī[1] whose sister Kṣatriyāṇī Triśalā was the mother of Mahāvīra, the founder of Jainism. In a Tibetan life of the Buddha, her name is Śrībhadrā[2] and in some places, she is named Maddā.[3] This lady, however, is usually called Vaidehī in the Buddhist books, and from her Ajātaśatru is frequently designated as Vedehiputto[4] or the son of the Videha princess. In the commentary on the Saṃyutta Nikāya, III. 2. sections 4-5, Buddhaghosa gives an alternative meaning of the word *Vedeha* in Vedehiputta by resolving it "into veda-iha, vedena-ihati or intellectual effort." He says that here the other meaning deriving the expression from Videha, the country, is not admissible. Some of the commentaries, as for example, those on

Bimbisara's marriage with a Licchavi girl.

1. Jacobi, Jaina Sūtras, S. B. E. Vol. XXII, Intro. pp. XIII.
2. Ibid, p. XIII, note 3.
3. Mrs. Rhys Davids and S. Sumaṅgala Thera. *The Book of the Kindred Sayings*, pt. I. p. 38, n. I.
4. *Saṁyutta Nikāya*, pt. II, p. 218.

Thusa and Tacchasūkara Jātakas,[1] state that Ajātaśatru's mother was a sister of the king of Kośala. Here the commentators have evidently made a confusion between the two queens of Bimbisāra. Buddhaghosa himself in other passages[2] has taken the more natural sense of the word but sometimes, as here, he has been misled into a fanciful interpretation.

The Divyāvadana speaks of Ajātaśatru as Vaidehiputra in one of the Avadānas[3] and in another place,[4] it states, "At Rājagṛha reigns the King Biṃbisāra. Vaidehī is his Mahādevī (or chief queen) and Ajātaśatru, his son and prince." There can, therefore, be no doubt that the Videha princess was the mother of Ajātaśatru. The Tibetan Dulva gives the name of Vāsavī to Ajātaśatru's mother and narrates a story which cannot be traced in the Pāli Buddhist books. We give here the story for what it is worth :—"Sakala, a minister of king Virudhaka of Videha, had been obliged to flee from his country on account of the jealousy of the other ministers of the king ; so he went to Vaiśālī together with his two sons, Gopāla and Sinha. Sakala soon became a prominent

1. Fausboll, III., 121 & IV, 342.

2. Commentary on Dīgha, I. 47, on Majjhima N. I, 125, on Saṁyutta N. II., 215. quoted by Mrs. Rhys Davids in "The Book of the Kindred Sayings, part I. p. 109. f.

3. *Divyāvadāna*, (Cowell & Neil), p. 55.

4. Ibid, p. 545. "Rājagṛhe Rājā Bimbisāro rājyaṁ kārayati.... tasya Vaidehī Mahādevī Ajātaśatruh putraḥ kumāro,"

citizen in Vaiśālī, and after a while he was elected Nāyaka. His two sons married at Vaiśālī, and Sinha had a daughter whom they called Vāsavī ; it was foretold that she would bear a son who would take his father's life, set the diadem on his own head, and seize the sovereignty for himself. Sinha's wife bore him, moreover, another daughter, whom they called Upavāsavī, and the seers declared that she would bear a son endowed with excellent qualities."

"Gopāla was fierce and of great strength, so he ravaged the parks of the Licchavis. To restrain him, the popular assembly gave him and his brother a park ; and thus it is said by the sthaviras in the sūtras, 'The Blessed One went out from Vaiśālī to the sala forest of Gopāla and Sinha."

"When Sakala died, the people appointed Sinha, his son, Nāyaka ; and Gopāla slighted at this, departed from Vaiśālī and took up his residence at Rājagṛha in Magadha where he became the first minister of Bimbisāra."

"A little later on, king Bimbisāra married Vāsavī, Gopāla's niece, and as she was of a family from Videha, she became known as Vaidehī. After a while she bore a son, who on account of the prediction made to his mother, received the name of Adjātaśatru, or the enemy (while) not (yet) born."[1]

---

1. Rockhill, *Life of the Buddha*, pp. 63-64.

Prof. D. R. Bhāndārkar holds that "this matrimonial alliance was a result of the peace concluded after the war between Bimbiśāra and the Licchavis[1] and that "Bimbisāra thus appears to have siezed Magadha after expelling the Vajjis beyond the Ganges."[2] The only evidence, however, that he has put forward in support of these theories is that Vaiśālī is spoken of, in an early Buddhist work, the Suttanipāta,[3] as *Māgadham puram*. This may be an expression loosely applied to Vaiśālī after its conquest by Ajātaśatru and even admitting that it speaks of an earlier time, it is too frail a reed on which to hang the whole theory of Bimbisāra wresting Magadha from the Licchavis. There seems to have some basis, however, to conclude that there was a war between Bimbisāra and the Licchavis, as such a war is referred to incidentally in the Tibetan Dulva. We shall quote the whole passage from Rockhill's *Life of the Buddha* in as much as the story traces the birth of Abhaya, another son of Bimbisāra, also by a Licchavi woman. The Dulva says, "There lived at Vaiśālī a Licchavi named Mahānāman. From a kadali tree in an āmra grove in his park was born a girl, lovely to look upon, perfect in all parts of

Birth of Abhaya, son of Bimbisara by a Licchavi woman.

1. Carmichael Lectures, 1918, p. 74.
2. Ibid, p. 73.
3. (New edition) P. T. S., p. 194.

her body, and he called her name Âmrapālī. When she was grown up, as there was a law of Vaiśālī by which a perfect woman was not allowed to marry, but was reserved for the pleasures of the people, she became a courtezan. Bimbisāra, King of Magadha, heard of her through Gopāla; he visited her at Vaiśālī, though he was at war with the Licchavis, and remained with her seven days. Âmrapālī became with child by him, and bore him a son whom she sent to his father. The boy approached the king fearlessly and climbed up to his breast which caused the king to remark, 'This boy seems not to know fear'; so he was called Abhaya or fearless."[1] This story which makes Abhaya or Abhayakumāra, as the Jaina books have it, a son of Ambapālī, the courtezan of Vaiśālī, is not vouchsafed by the Pāli Books where her son through Bimbisāra, is called Vimala-Kondañña who became a Bhikkhu and whose preachings are said to have given her a deep spiritual insight.[2]

The Licchavis and King Prasenajit of Kosala,

The Licchavis appear to have been on friendly terms with king Prasenajit of Kośala who speaks of them as his friends in a passage in the Majjhima Nikāya. Prasenajit proceeded to arrest Aṅgulimāla, the murderer, and on his way

1. Rockhill. *Life of the Buddha*, p. 64.
2. *Psalms of the Sisters*, pp. 120-121, *Psalms of the Brethren*, p. 65.

met the Buddha who enquired whether he was going to fight with Bimbisāra of Magadha or the Licchavis of Vaiśālī or some other rival kings; thereupon Prasenajit replied that all of them were his friends.[1]

The Licchavis and the Mallas.

The relation of the Licchavis with their neighbours, the Mallas, also seems to have been, in general, friendly as is evidenced by the Mallas standing by the Licchavis against their common foe Ajātaśatru. The Jaina books also speak of nine Malla chiefs and nine Licchavi chiefs showing reverence to Mahāvīra at the time of his passing away from the world. There were, however, occasional hostilities, as is shown by the story of Bandhula, a mallian prince.

In the Bhaddasāla Jātaka,[2] we find that the Licchavis hearing the sound of the chariot of Bandhula put a strong guard by the side of the tank. Bandhula came down from his chariot and put the guards to flight and in the tank he bathed his wife and gave her water to drink and put her in his chariot and then left the town. The Licchavi kings were informed and they were angry. Five hundred Licchavis mounting as many chariots followed the general. They were asked not to follow but they heeded not

1. *Majjhima Nikāya*, P. T. S. Vol. II, pp. 100-101. Aṅgulimāla Suttam.

2. Jātaka, (Cowell's edition), Vol. IV, p. 94.

and followed on and on till they were half dead. Bandhula said, "I cannot fight with the dead." They afterwards died. Bandhula, the mallian general, at last became victorious.

The Licchavis and Ajatasatru

We next come to the relations of the Licchavis with Ajātaśatru, the son and successor of Bimbisāra. It cannot be expected that the man whose greed for power and position did override even the natural instinct of regard for his father's life, would show any tender feeling towards his mother's relations. On the other hand, he must have felt from the very beginning that the Licchavis formed the greatest bar to the realisation of his idea of Magadhan expansion, and we find him taking the dreadful resolve, "I will root out these Vaggians, mighty and powerful though they be, I will destroy these Vaggians, I will bring these Vaggians to utter ruin."[1]

Downfall of the Licchavis.

The city of Vaiśālī reached the zenith of prosperity but her prosperity could not be sustained by the Vajjians, who, it seems, attacked Ajātaśatru, King of Magadha, many times. This enraged him very much and in order to baffle their attempts, two of his ministers, Sunīdha and Vassakāra, built a fort at

1. Buddhist Suttas, S. B. E., Vol. XI, pp. 1 & 2.

Pāṭaligāma [1] and at last Ajātaśatru annihilated the Vajjians. Prof. Rhys Davids[2] holds that it was some political motive which led him to do so but the learned doctor is silent as to what that motive was.

We find two reasons which cannot, on any account, be called political motive, and which go to show how the destiny of the Vajjians completely changed with little hope of restoration.

Ajātaśatru was not on friendly terms with the Licchavis. He was under the impression that his foster brother, Abhaya, (son of Bimbisāra by Ambapālī, a courtezan of Vaiśālī) had Licchavi blood in him and he liked the Licchavis very much. At this time the Licchavis were gaining strength day by day, and Ajātaśatru thought that if Abhaya sided with them it would be very difficult for him to cope with the Licchavis. So he made up his mind to do away with them.

In the Sumaṅgalavilāsinī,[3] we find that

---

1. Buddhist Suttas (S. B. E.) Vol. XI. p. 18.
2. Buddhist India, p. 12.
3. "Gaṅgāyaṁ kira ekaṁ paṭṭanagāmaṁ nissāya aḍḍha Ajātasattuno āṇā, addha yojanaṁ Licchavīnaṁ. Ettha pana āṇāpavattiṭṭhānaṁ hotiti attho. Tatrāpi ca pabbatapādato mahogghabhaṇḍaṁ otarati. Taṁ sutvā ajjayāmi aveyāmiti. Ajātasattuno saṁvidahantassava Licchavi-rājāno samaggā sammodamānā puretaraṁ gantvā sabbaṁ gaṇhanti. Ajātasattu pacchā āgantvā taṁ pavattiṁ ñatvā kujjhitvā gacchati. Te puna saṁvacchare pi tath'eva karonti. Attha so balavā ghāṭajāto tadā evaṁ akāsi. Tato cintesi, 'gaṇena saddhiṁ yuddhaṁ nāma bhāriyam. Ekopi moghappahāro nāma n' atthi." (Suttanta Piṭaka, Mahāvagga Atthakathā, edited by U. Pe. p. 96.)

there was a port near the Ganges extending over a yojana, half of which belonged to Ajātaśatru and half to the Licchavis and their orders were obeyed in their respective yojanas. There was a mountain not far from it and at the foot of the mountain there was a mine of precious gems. Ajātaśatru was late in coming there and the avaricious Licchavis took away all the precious gems. When Ajātaśatru came and learnt that all the precious gems had been taken away by the Licchavis, he grew angry and left the place. This happened also in the succeeding year. He having sustained a heavy loss thought that there must be a fight between him and the Licchavis. He realised, however, that the Licchavis being numerically stronger, he would fail to carry out his purpose. So he conceived the design of destroying the independence of the Licchavis by sowing seeds of dissension. Formerly, the Licchavis were not luxurious but very strenuous and exerting, so Ajātaśatru could not get an opportunity of subduing them. He sent Vassakāra, one of his ministers, to the Buddha who predicted that in future the Licchavis would be delicate, having soft hands and feet, would use very luxurious and soft beds with soft pillows made of cotton, would sleep till sunrise[1] and further declared: "By no other means will the Vajjians be

1. Saṁyutta Nikāya, (P. T. S.) pt. II., p 268.

overcome but by propitiating them with tributes or dissolving the subsisting union." Vassakāra returned from the Buddha and repeated the declaration of the ascetic Gotama. The Rājā did not agree to propitiate the Vajjians with tributes as that would diminish the number of elephants and horses. So he decided to break up their union and Vassakāra advised him to convene a meeting of the councillors to bring up some discussions regarding the Vajjians when in the midst of the sitting; he (Vassakāra) would quit the council after offering a remonstrance saying "Mahārāja, what do you want with them ? Let them occupy themselves with the agricultural and commercial affairs of their own (realm)." Then he said to Ajātaśatru, "Mahārājạ ! completely cut off all my hair, bringing a charge against me for interdicting your discussion without either binding or flogging me. As I am the person by whom ramparts and ditches of your capital were formed and as I know the strong and the weak, high and low parts (of your fortification), I will tell the Vajjians that I am able to remove any obstacle you can raise."

The Rājā acted up to the advice of his minister, Vassakāra. The Vajjians heard of the departure of Vassakāra and some of them decided not to allow him to cross the river while others observed, "He (Ajātaśatru) has so treated him because he advocated our cause" ; that being the case, they said (to the guards who went to stop him) "fellows, let him come." Accordingly, the guards permitted him to come in.

Now Vassakāra being questioned by the Vajjians told them why he was so severely punished for so slight an offence, and that he was there a Judicial Prime Minister. Then the Vajjians offered him the same post which he accepted and very soon he acquired reputation for his able administration of justice and the youths of the (Vajji) rulers went to him to have their training at his hands.

Vassakāra, on a certain day, taking aside one of the Licchavi rulers (mysteriously) asked, "Do people plough a field ?" "Yes, they do; by coupling a pair of bullocks together." On another occasion, taking another Licchavi aside he significantly asked, "With what curry did you eat (your rice) ?" and said no more. But hearing the answer, he communicated it to another person. Then upon a subsequent occasion, taking another Licchavi aside, he asked him in a whisper, "Art thou a mere beggar ?" He enquired, "Who said so ?" and the Brahmin, Vassakāra, replied : "That Licchavi." Again upon another occasion, taking another aside, he enquired, 'Art thou a cowherd ?' and on being asked who said so, he mentioned the name of some other Licchavi. Thus by speaking something to one person which had not been said by anyother person he succeeded in bringing about a disunion among the rulers in course of three years so completely that none of them would tread the same road together. When matters stood thus he caused the tocsin to be sounded as usual. The Licchavi rulers disregarded their call saying: "Let the rich and the valiant assemble. We are beggars and cowherds." The Brahmin sent a mission to the Rājā saying "this is the proper time, let him come quickly." The Rājā on hearing this announcement, assembled his forces by beat of drum and started. The Vajjians on receiving intimation thereof sounded the tocsin declaring "Let us not allow the Rājā to cross the river." On hearing this also they refused to meet together saying, "Let the valiant rulers go." Again the tocsin was sounded and it was thus declared: "Let us not allow the Rājā to enter the city, let us defend ourselves with closed gates." No one responded to the call. Ajātaśatru entered by the wide open gates, and came back after putting them to great calamities.[1] Thus the Magadhan kingdom was very much extended during the reign of Ajātaśatru.

Of the subsequent history of the Licchavis we know very little. But this much is certain that they were not exterminated by Ajātaśatru.

1. G. Turnour, An Examination of the Pāli Buddhistical Annals, No. V., J. A. S. B. Dec. 1838, pp. 994. f.—996. f.

What Ajātaśatru seems to have succeeded in doing, was that the Licchavis had to accept his suzerainty and pay him revenue, but they must have been independent in the matter of internal management and maintained in tact the ancient democratic institutions of personal liberty. Kauṭilya speaks of them two centuries after Ajātaśatru as living under a saṃgha form of government, and the same learned author advises the king Candra Gupta Maurya to seek the help of these saṃghas which on account of their unity and concord were almost unconquerable. This shows that the Licchavis though they might have been forced to acknowledge the suzerainty of Magadha, enjoyed a great deal of independence under Candra Gupta. There can be no doubt that under his grandson Aśoka, the Licchavis accepted his suzerainty.

The Licchavis and Candra Gupta Maurya.

The Licchavis and Asoka.

We next meet the Licchavis in Manu's Code[1] the recension of which was made, according to Dr. Bühler,[2] sometime during the period 200 B.C.—200 A.D.; in our opinion the date is likely to fall within the period of a Brāhmanic revival under Puṣyamitra Sunga, so that about a century after the time of Aśoka, we find the

The Licchavis in Manu's Code.

1. Manu, X. 22.
2. Bühler, Laws of Manu, S. B. E., Intro, p. CXVII.

Licchavis still living in Northern India as a Kṣatriya people. We do not hear of them again until the fourth century A. D. when their name appears on the records of the Imperial Guptas.

The Licchavis and the Imperial Guptas.

At the beginning of the fourth century A. D., a son-in-law of the Licchavi family, a son of Ghaṭotkaca Gupta, Candra Gupta I established a new kingdom.[1] A gold coin was introduced under the name of Candra Gupta I. On one side of it were incised the figures of Candragupta and his queen Kumāradevī and the words "Candragupta" and "Sree Kumāradevī" in the Brāhmī character of the fourth century A. D., and on the other side were engraved the figure of Laxmī, the goddess of Fortune seated on a lion and the word "Licchavayaḥ."[2] Mr. Allen presumes that Samudragupta was born in a Licchavi family and to keep up the memory of the father, Candragupta, and mother, Kumāradevī, the coin was issued. It is not improbable that the inscription *Licchavayaḥ* which occurs in Candragupta's gold coins together with the name of his queen Kumāradevī may signify that she belonged to a royal family of the Licchavis previously reigning at Pāṭaliputra[3], (modern Patna) which seems to have been the original capital of the Gupta Empire. A similar opinion

1. R. D. Banerjee, *Prācina Mudrā*, p. 121.
2. Ibid, p. 122.
3. Rapson's Indian coins, p. 24.

is also held by Dr. V. A. Smith who says that in early days of Buddhism, Candra Gupta, a local rājā at or near Pataliputra, married Kumāra devī, a princess belonging to the Licchavi clan, in or about the year 308.[1] In ancient times the Licchavis of Vaiśāli had been the rivals of the kings of Pāṭaliputra. Candra Gupta's position was elevated through his Licchavi connections from the rank of a local chief.[2] His son and successor often felt pride in describing himself as the son of the daughter of the Licchavis.[3] Before his death, his son by the Licchavi princess, Samudra Gupta, was selected by him as his successor.[4]

The Nepal inscriptions point out that there were two distinct houses, one of which known as the Thākuri family, is mentioned in the Vaṃsāvalī but is not recorded in the inscriptions; and the other one was the Licchavi or the Sūrya-vaṃsī family which issued its charters from the house or palace called Mānagṛiha and used an era uniformly with the Gupta epoch.[5] Thus we find that the Licchavis were not inferior to the Imperial Guptas so far as rank and power were concerned.[6] Their friendly relations with the Guptas were established by the marriage of Candra Gupta I with Kumāradevī, a daughter of the Licchavis.

---

1. V. A. Smith, Early History of India (3rd Ed.) p. 279.
2. Ibid, p. 280. 3. Ibid, p. 280.
4. V. A. Smith, Early History of India, (3rd Ed) p. 281.
5. Fleet, Corpus Inscriptionum Indicarum, Vol. III, p. 133.
6. Ibid, p. 135.

PART II.

Part II.

CHAPTER I.

The Videhas.

The Videhas are mentioned as a people in the Brāhmaṇa portion of the Vedas. That part of the country where they lived appears, however, to have been known by the name of Videha in the still more ancient times of the Saṃhitās. The Saṃhitās of the Yajurveda mention the cows of Videha which appear to have been specially famous in ancient India in the Vedic times.[1]

Vedic Evidence.

Coming to the Páurāṇic age we find Ramcandra, the hero of the Rāmāyaṇa, marrying Vaidehī, the reputed daughter of Janaka, King of Mithila.[2] In the Mahābhārata, Videha is mentioned in connection with the Rājsūya Jagña when Bhīma conquered it.[3]

Videha in the Epics.

"In the Brahmanic period, the chief nations of nothern India were the Kurus, the Pāñcālas,

---

1. The commentator of the Taittiriya Saṁhitā explains the adjective Vaidehī by Vaśiṣṭha-deba-Sambandhinī, 'having a splendid body (see Vedic Index Vol. II, p. 298 and Keith's Veda of Black Yajus School Vol. I, p. 138)

2. R. Bālakāṇḍaṁ (Bombay edition, Chap. 73)

3, M. Sabhāparva, Chap. 28. p 241. (Vangabāsī Edition)

the Kośalas, the Kāśīs and the Videhas. The Kurus and the Pāñcālas were so intimately connected with each other that they practically constituted one nation. The Kośalas, the Kāśīs and the Videhas formed a sort of confederacy and their relations with the Kurupāñcāla peoples were not perhaps always very friendly."[1] It may be noted here that of the eight confederate clans in Buddhist India forming the Vriji group, the Licchavis and the Videhas were the most important.[2]

Kosala-Kasi-Videha confederacy.

According to Julius Eggeling, there lived to the east of the Madhyadeśa at the time of the redaction of the Brāhmaṇas, a confederacy of kindred peoples known as the Kośalavidehas occupying a position no less important than that of the Kurupāñcālas. He further states that the legendary account is that these people claimed Videgha Māthava to be their common ancestor and they are said to have been separated from each other by the River Sadānīrā (corresponding to either the modern Gandak or Karatoyā according to Sāyaṇa). In his opinion the Videhan country was in those days the extreme east of the land of the Aryans.[3] Dr. Weber

Kosala-Videha confederacy.

1. Dr. P. Banerjee, Public Administra in Ancient India, pp. 54-55.
2. Dr. Rhys Davids, Buddhist India, p. 26.
3. S'atapatha Brāhmaṇa, S. B. E. Vol. XII, Intro. XLII-XLIII.

points out that the Aryans apparently pushed further up the River Saraswatī led by Videgha Māthava and his priest as far east as the River Sadānīrā which formed the eastern boundary of the Videhas or more probably the Gandakī which was the boundary between the Kośalas and the Videhas.[1]

Origin of the name.

The country is said to have derived its name from this King Videgha Māthava or Videha Mādhava who introduced the sacrificial fire; and according to some, this introduction of the sacrificial fire is symbolical of the inauguration of the Brāhmanical faith in that region.

The Viṣṇu Purāṇa, however, gives a different account of the origin of the name Videha and also that of Mithilā, the capital. It relates that Vaśiṣṭha having performed the sacrifice of Indra proceeded to Mithilā to commence the sacrifice of King Nimi. On reaching there he found that the king had engaged Gautama to perform the sacrificial rites. Seeing the King asleep he cursed him thus: "The King Nimi will be bodiless (Videha; vi-vigata, deha) in as much as he having rejected me has engaged Gautama." The king being awake cursed Vaśiṣṭha saying that Vaśiṣṭha too would perish as he had cursed a sleeping king. Ṛṣis churned the dead body of Nimi. As a result of the

1. S. B. E. Vol. XII, p. 104. F.

churning, a child was born, afterwards known as Nimi, his birth being due to churning.

Videha was 24 yojanas in length from the River Kouśiki to the River Gandakī and 16 yojanas in breadth from the Ganges to the Himalayas.[1]

Its area.

The capital of Videha was Mithilā situated about 35 miles north-west from Vesāli.[2] The distance between Mithilā and Ajodhyā may be gathered from the fact that during the reign of Janaka, King of Videha, when Viśwāmitra came to Mithilā with Rāma and Lakṣaṇa, it took them four days to reach Mithilā from Ajodhyā. They took rest for one night only at Viśālā on their way.[3] Mithilā was founded by king Mithi better known as Janaka. According to the Bhaviṣya Purāṇa, Nimi's son, Mithi, founded a beautiful city near Tirhut which was named Mithilā after him. From the fact of his having founded the city, he came to be known as Janaka.[4] The Mahāgovinda Suttanta of the Dīgha Nikāya gives another account of its origin and states that Mithilā of the Videhas was built by Govinda.[5]

Mithila, the capital.

1. Vrihad Viṣṇu Purāṇa, "Kauśikiṁ tu samāravya......Mithilā nāma nagarī tatraste loka viśrutā."

2. Rhys Davids, Buddhist India, p. 26.

3. Rāmāyaṇa (Vangavāsī) 1-3.

4. Bhaviṣyapurāṇa, "Nimeḥ putrastu tatraiva......Pūrijanana sāmarthāt Janakaḥ saca kirtitaḥ."

5. P. T. S., Vol. II., p. 235.

It is stated in the Jātaka that the city of Mithilā, the capital of the Videhans, was 7 leagues and the kingdom of Videha 300 leagues in extent.[1] It was the capital of the kings Janaka and Makhādeva in the district now called Tirhut.[2] The city of Mithilā in Jambudvīpa had plenty of elephants, horses, chariots, oxen, sheep and all kinds of wealth of this nature together with gold, silver, gems, pearls and other precious things.[3] From a Jātaka description we learn that the kingdom of Videha had 16,000 villages, storehouses filled, and 16,000 dancing girls.[4] Magnificent royal carriages were drawn by four horses. The Videhan king was seen seated in a carriage drawn in state around his capital.[5]

In the Si-Yu-Ki (Buddhist Records of the Western World), we find that the Chinese traveller, Hiuen Tsiang, describing the kingdom of Fo-li-shi (Vrijji) says that the capital of the country is Chen-shu-na. At the foot of the page (p. 77) we find a note by the translator who calls our attention to the fact that the country of the Vṛijis was that of the confederated eight tribes of the people called

1. Jātaka (Cowell's edition) Vol. III, p. 222.
2. Buddhist India, p. 30.
3. Beal's Romantic Legend of Sākya Buddha, p. 30.
4. Jātaka, Vol. III., p. 222.
5. Ibid., Vol. II., pp. 27-28.

the Vṛijis. He quotes V. de St. Martin who connects the name Chen-shu-na with Janaka and Janakapur, the capital of Mithilā,[1] which, according to V. Smith, corresponds to the modern Champārān and Darbhanga districts.[2]

Videha, a trade centre.

From a very early time, Videha became a trade-centre. At the time of Buddha Gautama we find people coming from Sāvatthi to Videha to sell their articles. When the Buddha was at Sāvatthi, a disciple of his, who was an inhabitant of Sāvatthi, took cart-loads of articles and went to Videha to trade. There he sold his articles and filled the carts with the articles got in exchange and then proceeded towards Sāvatthi. When he was proceeding through a forest, one wheel of a cart broke down. Then another person who had gone out of his own village with an axe to cut down trees reached the very spot while wandering in the forest. He saw the disciple dejected on account of the breaking of the wheel. Taking pity on the traveller he cut down a tree, made a strong wheel out of it and fixed it to the cart and thus got him out of the trouble. The latter then succeeded in reaching Sāvatthi.[3]

---

1. Beal's Records of the Western World, Vol. II. p. 71.N.
2. History of India, pp. 400-401.
3. Dhammapāla's Paramatthadīpanī on the Therīgāthā pt. III, pp. 277-278

The Videhans were a charitable people. Many institutions of charity were in existence. Daily 600,000 pieces were spent in alms-giving.[1] We find it stated in the Makhādeva Jātaka how a Videhan king, when he renounced the worldly life, gave a village to his barber which fetched him much.

1. The people—charitable.

The Jātaka stories occasionally make extravagant demands upon popular credence as when they relate how the average length of human life at the time of the Buddha Gautama was thirty thousand years. More fortunate than the average mortal, King Makhādeva of Mithilā had a lease of life for 84,000 years, in the earlier portion of which he amused himself as a royal prince and later on was appointed a viceroy, and last of all he became a king.

We, however, come to a more sober estimate when we find it related that there lived in Mithilā, a Brahmin named Brahmāyu, aged 120 years, who was well versed in the Vedas, Itihāsas, Vyākaraṇa, Lokāyata and was endowed with all the marks of a great man.[2]

2. Long-lived.

Polygamy appears to have been in vogue among the kings of Videha. Brahmadatta,

---

1. Jātaka (Cowell), Vol. IV. p. 224.
2. Majjhima Nikāya, Vol. II. pt. I. pp. 133-134.

King of Benares, had a daughter named Sumedhā whom he declined to give in marriage to a prince who had a large number of wives, fearing that her co-wives would make her life very miserable. So he thought that he would marry his daughter to a prince who would wed her alone and take no other wife.[1]

3. Polygamous.

We read in one of the Jātakas that in Videha the people reproached the king for his childlessness and suggested to the king various devices which could be accepted or rejected by the king who could ask for the advice of the people as to what to do.[2]

In the past when king Videha was reigning at Mithilā, his queen bore him a son who grew up and was educated at Taxilā.[3] Taxilā was the seat of learning where the Videhan princes, like the princes of the other states,[4] used to receive instruction.

Royal princes educated at Taxila.

The kings of Mithilā were men of high culture. Janaka, the great Rājarṣi of the Brāhmaṇic period, had received Brahmavidyā or Âtmavidyā from the great sage Yāgñavalkya, the

1. Jātaka., Vol. IV., pp. 198-205.
2. Ibid. Vol. V., pp. 141-142.
3. Ibid, Vol. II, p. 27.
4. See my paper "Taxilā as a seat of learning in the Pāli Literature." J. A. S. B., N. S. Vol., XII, 1916.

celebrated author of the Yāgñavalkyasaṃhitā.[1]

Videhan kings' love of learning.

In the Buddhist age, we find Sumitra, king of Mithilā, devoted to the practice and study of true law.[2] King Videha of Mithilā had four sages to instruct him in law.[3]

Magadha and Videha's contact with Vedic culture.

A German scholar has asserted on the authority of the Brāhmaṇa texts and the Dharmaśāstras that Magadha and Videha came late in contact with Vedic culture and were never influenced so much by it as the western people.[4] Assuming that it is so, we find that in the later Mantra period, Videha must have been organised so far as to take a leading part in Vedic culture, and the Śatapatha Brāhmaṇa clearly indicates that the great spiritual and intellectual lead offered by Samrāt Janaka and Ṛṣi Yāgñavalkya had to be accepted by the whole of Northern India. Ṛṣis from the Madra country on the north western frontiers and from the Kurupāñcāla regions flocked to the court of Janaka and took part in the discussions held about the supreme Brahman and had to admit the superior knowledge of Yājñavalkya.

Once a great sacrifice known as the Vahu-

1. Anargha Rāghava, (Nirṇayasāgara Edition), p. 117.
2. Romantic Legend of Sākya Buddha, p. 30.
3. Jātaka, Vol. VI, p. 156.
4. Vrihat Araṇyaka Upaniṣad pp. 115-116 (Anandāśrama Ed.)

Sacrifices in Videha.

dakṣiṇā was performed by Janaka,[1] King of Videha. The Brāhmins of Kuru and Pāncāla attended it. The king was desirous of knowing who amongst them had realised the supreme Brahman. He had 1,000 cows brought before him and ten padas (of gold) were fastened to each pair of horns and it was proclaimed that such a Brāhmin would take them all. When no other sage ventured to take them, the great sage Yājña-valkya asked his own Brahmacārins to take the cows.[2] Sacrifices performed by the Videhan kings have been referred to in the Jātaka stories. Goats were sacrificed in the name of religion.[3] Ikṣāku's son, Nimi, a king of the solar race, performed a sacrifice for a thousand years with the help of Vaśiṣṭha who had previously officiated as high-priest at a certain sacrifice lasting for 500 years performed by Indra. On the completion of that sacrifice, Vaśiṣṭha went to Mithilā to commence the sacrifice of king Nimi.[4] Viśwāmitra said to Rāma who was with Lakṣaṇa, "Dear, we are going to Mithilā, of which Janaka is the ruler. After attending the

1. Described by Aśwaghosa as one who being a householder attained merit leading to final bliss.
2. Vrihadāraṇyaka Upaniṣad, pp. 105-106 (Anandāśrama Ed.)
3. Jātaks, Vol IV, p. 220.
4. Viṣṇupurāṇa. p. 246. (Vangabāsi Edition.)

great sacrifice of Janaka, we shall make for Ajodhyā."[1]

Once Nimi, King of Videha, was looking down at the street through an open window of the palace. A hawk was then seen flying up into the air, taking some meat from the meat market. The bird was molested by some vultures and other birds which began to peck it with their beaks. It had to give up the piece of meat as their pecking was too much for it and the same piece of meat was then taken up by another bird which met with the same fate and dropped it and a third took it and was molested in the same way. Thereupon the following thoughts arose in the king's mind :—'The possessor was unfortunate and the relinquisher was happy ; sorrow befell a person who indugled in the pleasures of the senses but happiness was the lot of the man who renounced them ; as he had 16,000 women, he ought to live in happiness ; but the pleasures of the senses should be renounced like the hawk relinquishing the morsel of flesh'. Considering this, wise as he was, he realised the three properties of blessedness and gained spiritual illumination and reached the wisdom of Paccekabuddha.[2]

Story of Nimi, king of Videha.

1. Adhyātma Rāmāyaṇa Bālkāṇḍa, Ch. VII. p.68. (Kālisaṅkara Vidyāratṇa's edition.)
2. Jātaka, Vol III, p. 230.

Another Jātaka story relates that Videha, King of Videha, and Bodhisatto, King of Gāndhāra, were on friendly terms though they never met each other. Once on the fast day of the full-moon, the king of Gāndhāra took the vow of the commands (a vow to keep the five moral precepts) and sitting on a royal throne prepared for him, he delivered before his ministers a discourse on the substance of the law. At that moment Rāhu was overshadowing the full moon's orb so that the moon's light became dim by an eclipse. The ministers told the king that the moon had been seized by Rāhu. The king observing the phenomenon thought that all the trouble came from outside; his royal retinue was nothing but a trouble and that it was not proper that he should lose his light like the moon seized by Rāhu. He then made over his kingdom to his ministers and took to a religious life and having attained transcendental faculty, he spent the rainy season in the Himalayan region, devoting himself to the delight of meditation.

King Bodhisatta of Gandhara.

The king of Videha when he heard of the religious life of the king of Gāndhāra abdicated the throne of Mithilā and went to the Himalayan region and became hermit. The two ex-kings lived together in peace and friendliness without knowing each other's antecedents. The ascetic

King Videha of Videha.

of Videha waited upon the ascetic of Gāndhāra. One day they saw the moon's light destroyed. The former asked the master (the ascetic of Gāndhāra) as to the cause of it. He was told by the master that all trouble came from outside like the trouble to the moon seized by Rāhu and that he (the master) taking the moon's orb seized by Rāhu as his theme, had left his kingdom and taken to a religious life. Whereupon Videha recognised the ex-king of Gāndhāra who had surely seen the good of religious life and said that he had heard of it and had taken him as his ideal and left his kingdom to lead a religious life.[1]

King Makhadeva's renunciation.

We have already referred to the long life of King Makhādeva of Mithila. The story of his renunciation may be summarised in a few words. One day he asked his barber to inform him when any grey hair on his head would be noticed by him. One day the barber saw a grey hair and placed it on the hand of the king who after seeing it became mortified and thought that his days were numbered. His eldest son was sent for and was asked to take charge of the sovereignty. He became a recluse and lived in a grove which was named Makhādeva's mango-grove. He developed very high spiritual powers

1. Jātaka (Cowell's edition) Vol. III, pp. 222-223

and after death was reborn in the realm of Brahmā. Passing thence he became a king in Mithilā and once more became a hermit. He again came to the realm of Brahmā.[1] Sādhina, a righteous king in Mithilā, kept the five virtues and observed the fast-day vows. The king's virtue and goodness were praised by the princes of Heaven who sat in the "Justice-Hall" of Sakka. All the gods desired to see him. Accordingly Sakka ordered Mātali to bring Sādhina to heaven in his own chariot. Mātali went to the kingdom of Videha. It was then the day of the full moon. Mātali drove his celestial chariot side by side with the moon's disc. All people kept on shouting "See, two moons are in the sky." But the chariot came near them and they cried, "It is no moon but a chariot, a son of the gods it would seem. Surely

King Sadhina's story

1. Jātaka (Cowell). Vol. I, pp. 31-32.

In the Makhādeva Suttaṁ (Majjhima Nikāya Vol. II, pt. I pp.74-83), we find the same story with slight variations. The King of Mithilā named Makhādeva was very righteous and used to perform his duties towards the Samaṇas, the Brāhmaṇas, the householders and the citizens. He used to observe the Sabbath on the 8th, the 14th and the 15th day of the lunar month. He told his barber to find out grey hairs. After many years, the barber found out grey hairs on his head and informed him. The other details are the same. The last king Nimi was like Makhādeva. Indra with gods came to him and praised him very much. As soon as Nimi reached the Mote Hall of the gods, he was received cordially by Indra who again praised him in the midst of the assembly of gods. He was sent back to his kingdom in the celestial chariot.

the chariot is for our king, virtuous as he is." Mātali went to the king's door and made a sign that he (king) should ascend the chariot. The king after arranging for the distribution of alms went away with Mātali.

One half of the city of gods and 25 millions of nymphs and a half of the palace of Vaijayanta were given by Sakka to Sādhina. The king lived there in happiness for 700 years. But afterwards when his merits were exhausted, dissatisfaction arose in him and he did not wish to remain in heaven any longer. The king was carried to Mithilā where he distributed alms for seven days and on the 7th day he died and was reborn in the Heaven of Thirty-three.[1]

Story of King Suruci and his Concort, Sumedha.

Suruci, King of Mithilā, had a wife named Sumedhā who was childless. Sumedhā prayed for a son. On the first of the fifteenth day of the month, she took the eight-fold sabbath vows (Aṭṭhasilānī) against taking life, theft, impurity, lying, intoxicating liquors, eating at forbidden hours, worldly amusements and 'sat meditating upon virtues in a magnificent room upon a pleasant couch.' Sakka in the guise of a sage came into the king's park and stayed at the window of the bedchamber of Sumedhā. She on learning from her companions

1. Jātaka (Cowell), Vol. IV, pp. 224-227.

that Sakka would give the boon of a son to a virtuous woman, entreated him to favour her with it. Sakka asked her to sing her own praises in fifteen stanzas which she did to his satisfaction. Afterwards she was blessed with a child.[1]

Brahmayu, a learned Brāhmin.

In the Buddhist works other than the Jātakas we also find occasional mention of Mithilā, the ancient Videha capital. Brahmāyu, the learned Brāhmin of Mithilā already described above, heard of the nine qualities of the Tathāgata who was foremost among the beings of Deva Brahmā and Māra worlds, who used to preach Dharma and would bring good to mankind. He had a pupil named Uttara. Once he said to his pupil that the Buddha who was endowed with various good qualities ought to be seen. Thereupon he sent Uttara to Videha to see the Buddha who was then staying there. At first Uttara noticed thirty out of the thirty-two marks of a great man in Buddha. He followed him like a shadow for seven months and at last he was successful in noticing the remaining two marks. Confidence arose in him. He then went to his guru (preceptor) who, on being told every thing, went to the Enlightened

1. Jātaka (Cowell)Vol. IV., pp. 198-205.

one, and being fully satisfied, was converted along with his pupil to the new faith.[1]

Vāsiṭṭhī was reborn in the family of a clansman at Vaiśālī. She was given in marriage by her parents to a clansman's son of equal status.

Vasitthi and the Buddha.

She bore a son who, when able to run about, died. She was mad with grief. While the relatives were comforting the husband, she, unknown to her relatives and to her husband, ran away raving. At last she came to Mithilā and saw the Buddha walking along the next street, 'self-controlled and self-contained.' At the sight of the Lord she recovered the former sober state of her mind and soon attained saintship.[2]

Sundarī was reborn in a clansman's family. One day she gave alms to the Buddha and worshipped him. After various re-births, her knowledge had developed and she was,

Sundari and the Buddha.

at the time of Buddha Gautama, reborn at Benares as a daughter of a Brahmin named Sujāṭa. When she grew up, her younger brother died. Her father became overwhelmed with grief and met the therī Vāsiṭṭhī whom he asked how to get rid of sorrow. She informed him of the means of becoming free from grief. Knowing that the

1. Majjhima Nikāya, Vol. II pts: I & II. pp. 133-146. Brahmāyu-Suttaṁ.

2. Psalms of the Sisters. p. 79.

Master was at Mithilā, he went there and the Master taught him the Norm ; he entered the order and became an Arhat.[1]

Names of other Videhan Kings

There were other Videhan kings besides Janaka whose names are mentioned in one of the Ceylonese chronicles, the Mahāvamsa, viz, Sāgaradeva, Bharata, Angirasa, Ruci, Suruci, Patāpa, Mahāpatāpa, Sudassana, Neru, Mahāsammata, Mucala, Mahāmucala, two Kalyāṇas and others—all these princes who lived very long, dwelt at Mithilā.[2] King Satadhanu, son of Janaka, was born and reborn again and again in lower forms of existence because he had sexual intercourse with a naked woman on a fasting day. He ruled in Videha.[3]

Mithila in later times.

Coming down to far later times, we observe that during the reign of Mahipāladeva, Gāngeyadeva of the Cedi dynasty, attacked Goudrājya (the ancient name of Bengal) and occupied Mithilā.[4] We find the name of Nānyadeva at the top of the list in the royal family in the Nepāl Vaṃsāvalī. Nānyadeva is mentioned in the inscribed stone of Joypratāpmalla of Nepāl as the first king of Karṇāṭaka Rāj family.[5] He

1. Psalms of the sisters, p. 135.
2. Mahāvamsa, Ch. II, Geiger's translation, p. 10.
3. Viṣṇu Purāṇa, pt. III, Ch. XVIII, p, 217. (Vangabāsī Edition)
4. R. D. Banerjee, Vāṅgālār Itihāsa, Vol. I p. 224.
5. Ibid, p. 290.

founded the Karṇāṭaka dynasty at Miṭhilā. He was defeaṭed by Vijayasena.[1] A new era began with the coronation of Lakṣaṇadeva of Bengal. This era was known as Lakṣanābda or Lakṣmaṇ-saṃbad or Lasaṃ which was for a long time prevalent in Mithilā.[2]

Vardhamana Mahavira and Mithila.

Vardhamāna Mahāvīra, the great founder of Jainism, "a Videha, son of Videhadattā, a naṭive of Videha, a prince of Videha, had lived thirty years in Videha when his parents died."[3] Mithilā was his favourite resort. Here six monsoons were spent by him.[4]

Udayana, the Vaidehiputra.

Dr. D. R. Bhāndārkar says that from the two well-known works of Bhāṣa, the Svapnavāsa-vadaṭtā and Pratigñā Yaugand-harāyaṇa, Udayana, son of Saṭānīka and grandson of Sahasrāṇīka, appears to have belonged to the Bhārata family. He is called Vaidehiputra because his mother seems to have been the daughter of the King of Videha.[5]

King Bimbisāra married Vāsavī. As she

---

1. R. D. Banerjee, Vāñgālār Itihāsa, Vol. I., p. 290.
2. Ibid , p. 299.
3. Jaina Sūtras, Vol XXII, pt. I, p. 256.
4. S. B. E., Vol. XLV., p. 42.
5. Carmichael Lectures., pp. 58 and 59, Udayana is addressed as Vaidehiputr (S V. Act. 6, p. 68 , Ganapati Sāstrī's edition).

was of a Videhan family, she became known as Vaidehī. Shortly afterwards she bore a son, who, true to the prophecy made to his mother, got the name Ajātaśatru or "the enemy (while) not (yet) born."[1]

Ajatasatru the Vaidehiputra.

It is stated in the Amitāyurdhyāna Sūtra that Ajātaśatru arrested his father Bimbisāra at the instigation of Devadatta and confined him in a room with seven walls, declaring that none should approach him. Vaidehī, the chief Queen of Bimbisāra, who was very faithful to her husband, having purified herself by bathing and washing, having anointed her body with honey and ghee mixed with corn flour and having concealed the juice of grapes in the various garlands she wore, saved his life. Ajātaśatru enquired about his father and he was informed by the warder of the gate about what Vaidehī had done. This enraged him much and he wanted to kill his mother. At this the ministers remonstrated with him and he had to give up this idea. Vaidehī was kept in seclusion. She showed great respect to the Buddha who appeared before her and gave her a long discourse on peace and contentment.[2]

In Buddha's time the Videhans had a

1. Rockhill's Life of the Buddha, pp. 63-64.
2. S. B. E., Vol. XLIX., pp. 161-201.

republican form of government, the headman of which, as we find in the case of other republics, was called a Rājā. They were included in the great Vajjian confederation, which, according to Kauṭilya, was a corporation that lived by the title of a Rājā.[1] They had their Santhāgāra or the Mote Hall where the tribal meetings were held.

Political Constitution.

A minister of King Virudhaka of Videha named Sakala was compelled to flee to Vaiśālī from his own country owing to the jealousy of the other ministers. There he soon became a prominent citizen. Shortly afterwards he was elected Nāyaka.[2]

---

1. Arthaśāstra Translated by R. Shamaśāstry p. 455.
2. Rockhill, *Life of the Buddha*. p. 63.

CHAPTER II.

The Mallas.

The Mallas were a powerful people of eastern India at the time of Gautama, the Buddha. They are often mentioned both in the Buddhist and the Jaina works.

The country of the Mallas is spoken of in many passages in the Buddhist works as one of the sixteen "great countries" (Mahājanapadas).[1]

Mallian Country.

At the time we are speaking of, they appear to have been divided into two confederacies, one with headquarters at Pāvā and the other with headquarters at Kuśīnārā, as we see from the Mahāparinibbāṇa Suttanta.[2]

It is remarkable that to these two capital cities of the Mallas came the two great founders of Jainism and Buddhism to pass the last days of their sojourn here on earth and to rid this world of woe. The Kalpa Sūtra,[3] one of the Jaina canonical works, tells us how in the seventieth year of his life "in the fourth month of the rainy season, in the seventh fortnight, in the dark (fortnight) of Kārtick, on its fifteenth day, in the last night, in the town of Pāpā, in

Buddha and Mahavira.

---

1. Aṅguttara Nikāya. see. X L 11. 4. etc.
2. Dīgha Nikāya Vol. II p. 165.
3. § 123. S. B. E. XXII. pp. 264-265.

King Hastipāla's office of the writers, the venerable ascetic Mahāvīra died, went off, quitted the world, cut asunder the ties of birth, old age and death ; became a Siddha, a Buddha, a Mukta, a Maker of the end (to all misery), finally liberated, freed from all pains." This Pāpā of the Kalpa Sūtra is no other than Pāvā-Purī in the neighbourhood of the modern city of Bihār-Sharif in the Patna district in the province of Bihar and is even at the present day one of the chief places of pilgrimage to the Jains. We are further informed by the Kalpa Sūtra that to mark the passing away of the Great Jīna, nine Mallakis or Malla chiefs were among those that instituted an illumination on the day of the new moon, saying, "Since the light of intelligence is gone, let us make an illumination of material matter."[1]

Identification of Papa (Pava).

The Sangīti Suttanta of the Dīgha Nikāya informs us that the Buddha, accompanied by five hundred followers, was travelling in the Malla country and came to Pāvā, the Malla capital.[2] There he dwelt in the Mango-grove of Cunda, the Smith. Then a new Mote Hall of the Pāvā Mallas named Ubbhaṭaka had just been built and had not been occupied by any

Buddha at Cunda's mango-grove.

1. S. B. E. XXII, p. 266,
2. Dialogues of the Buddha., pt. III. p. 201.

body. They invited the Buddha to this freshly built council-hall saying, "Let Lord, the Exalted One, be the first to make use of it. That it has first been used by the Exalted One will be for the lasting good and happiness of the Pāvā Mallas."

Buddha's discourse on his doctrine.

At their request, the Buddha gave a discourse on his doctrine to the Mallas of Pāvā till late hours of the night "instructing, enlightening, inciting and inspiring them." They then went away and the Master 'laid himself down to rest.' It was also at this Mallian city of Pāvā that the Buddha ate his last meal at the house of Cunda, the Smith (Kumāraputta), and he was attacked with dysentery. Being ill the Exalted One went to the rival Mallian city of Kuśīnārā. When he felt that the last moment was fast approaching, he sent Ânanda with a message to the Mallas of Kuśīnārā who had then assembled in their Santhāgāra or Mote-Hall for some public affair. On receipt of the news, they flocked to the Śāla grove with their youngmen, girls and wives, 'being grieved and sad and afflicted at heart.' The venerable Ânanda caused them 'to stand in groups, each family in a group' and presented them to the Blessed one, saying, "Lord, a Malla of such and such a name with his children, his wives, his retinue and his

Kusinara.

Message to the Mallas of kusinara.

friends humbly bows down at your feet." In this way he presented them all to him.[1] Then after his last exhortations to the assembled brethren to work out their salvation with diligence, he entered into Parinirvāṇa. They then met together in their council-hall to devise some means of honouring the earthly remains of the Lord in a suitable manner and carried them with mirth and music to the shrine of the Mallas, called the Makuṭa-bandhana, to the east of their city and they treated the remains of the Tathāgata as they would treat the remains of a king of kings (Cakravarttī-Rājā).[2] When at last the cremation was over, they put out the funeral pyre with water scented with all sorts of perfumes and collected the bones which they placed in their Mote-Hall, surrounding them 'with a lattice work of spears and with a rampart of bows.'[3]

Honour to the Buddha.

Among the various clans that pressed their claims for a share of the remains were the Mallas of Pāvā, for the reason that they had a separate principality. They sent a messenger to the Mallas of Kuśīnārā, saying :—"The Exalted One was a Kṣatriya and so are we. We are worthy to receive a portion of the relics of the Exalted One. Over the remains of the

1, Dialogues of the Buddha, II. pp. 162-164.

2. Ibid., p. 182. 3. Ibid., pp. 186-187.

Exalted One will we put up a sacred cairn, and in his honour, will we celebrate a feast." Both the Mallas of Pāvā and Kuśīnārā erected stupas over their respective shares and celebrated feasts.

Stupas over the Buddha's relics.

The passage quoted above shows that the Mallas belonged to the Kṣatriya caste and in the Mahāparinibbāṇa Suttanta, they are repeatedly addressed by the Buddha as well as by Ânanda and others as Vāśeṭṭhas or Vāśiṣṭhas. The Mallas of Pāvā are also addressed as Vāseṭṭhas by the Buddha in the Sangīti Suttanta of the Dīgha Nikāya.[1] This shows that all the Mallas belonged to the Vaśiṣṭha gotra like the Licchavis. Like the Licchavis again the Mallas are mentioned by Manu to have been born of a Kṣatriya mother and of a Kṣatriya father who was a Vrātya, that is, who had not gone through the ceremony of Vedic initiation at the proper age.

Mallas—a Ksatriya tribe.

We are told in the Sabhāparva of the Mahābhārata that the second Pāṇḍava, Bhīmasena, during his expedition conquered the chief of the Mallas besides the country of Gopālakakṣa and the Northern Kośala territories.[2] Amongst the

The Mallas in the Mahabharata.

1. Dialogues of the Buddha., pt. II, pp. 162 ff.
2. Vangavāsī Edition, Vol. I. p. 241. Sabhā, Chap. 30. Sloka 3.

peoples inhabiting the different countries of India, the Bhīṣmaparva mentions the Mallas along with such East-Indian peoples as the Aṅgas, the Vaṅgas, the Kaliṅgas and others.[1]

From the Greek account of Alexander's invasion of India, we come across the name of Malloi, a warlike tribe, who resisted for a time the onslaught of Alexander. The Malloi was a race of independent Indians.[2]

There is a consensus of opinion among historians that the territory of the Malloi is situated in or near the Punjab. From the analogy of the names Malloi and Malla and from their warlike character, it may be said that they are of the same origin. But as we are not certain of any previous history of the Mallas during the time when Alexander invaded India, we cannot definitely say one way or the other.

When the Lord expressed to Ânanda his desire to die at Kuśinārā, Ânanda said to him,

Importance of Kusinara.

"Let not the Exalted One die in this little wattle-and-daub town, in this town in the midst of the jungle, in this branch township......" The Buddha repudiated it by saying that it was not so.

---

1. Vangavāsī Ed. Bhīṣmaparva., Chap. IX, Sloka 46, p. 822.
2. The invasion of India by Alexander the Great as described by Arrian, Curtius Diodoros, Plutarch & Justin by J. W. M' Crindle, p. 140.

Kusinara—Its identification.

The fact that the Buddha hastened to Kuśīnārā from Pāvā during his last illness proves that the journey did not take him long; but the description in the Mahāparinibbāṇa Suttanta does not enable us to make any accurate estimate of the distance between the two cities of the Mallas. Kuśīnārā has been identified by Cunningham with the village of Kasiā to the east of the Gorakhpur district[1] and this view has recently been strengthened by the fact that in the stūpa behind the Nirvāṇa temple, near this village, has been discovered a copperplate bearing the inscription [parini] rvāṇa-chaitya-tāmra-paṭṭa, or the copperplate of the parinirvāṇa-caitya. This identification appears to be correct, although the late Dr. Vincent. A. Smith would prefer to place Kuśīnārā in Nepal, beyond the first range of hills.[2] Professor Rhys Davids expresses the opinion that the territory of the Mallas of Kuśīnārā and Pāvā, "if we may trust the Chinese Pilgrims, was on the mountain slopes to the east of the Śākya land and to the north of the Vajjian confederation. But some would place their territory south of the Śākyas and east

1. Cunningham, Ancient Geography of India, pp. 430-433.

2. V. A. Smith—Early History of India p. 159. f. n. 5. Pargiter. J, R. A. S. 1913. p. 152.

of the Vajjians."[1] It is a considerable distance from Kāsiā in the Gorakhpur district to Pāwā-purī of the Jainas in the Patna district and one so ill as the Buddha was after his meal at the house of Cunda was not likely to walk such a distance on foot. Therefore, Pāvā of the Buddhist books appears to have been not very far from Kāsiā.

Anupiya, another Malla town.

The Cullavagga of the Vinaya Piṭaka mentions another town of the Mallas named Anupiyā[2] where the Buddha resided for some time. This Anupiyā may be the same as the mango-grove called Anupiya where Gautama spent the first seven days after his renunciation on his way to Rājagriha.[3]

Malla tawn Uruvelakappa.

A fourth town of the Mallas called Uruvelakappa is mentioned in the Aṅguttara Nikāya, where the Blessed one stayed for some time.[4] In its neighbourhood, there appears to have existed a wide forest called Mahāvana where the Buddha

1. Buddhist India, p. 26.

2. Cullavagga. VII. I. I. Vinaya Texts S. B. E. pt III. p. 224

3. Tasmiṁ eva padese Anupiyaṁ nāma ambavanaṁ atthi : tattha sattāhaṁ pabbajjāsukhena Vitināmetvā tiṁsayojanaṁ Maggaṁ padasā gantvā Rājagahaṁ pāvimi.. Introduction to the Jātakas, Fanaboll, Jātaka Vol 1. pp 65-66.

4. "Evaṁ me sutaṁ. Ekaṁ samayaṁ Bhagavā Mallikesu Viharati Uruvelakappaṁ nāma Mallikānaṁ nigamo." Saṁyutta Nikāya, pt. V. p. 228.

went alone for midday rest after his meal and where he met the Gahapati Tapussa.

Love of learning

That the Mallian princes had a love for learning is evident from the following incident. Bandhula, a son of a Mallian king of Kuśînārā, went to Taxila for education. There he sat at the feet of a great teacher along with Pasenadī of Kośala and Mahāli, a Licchavi prince of Vaiśālī. After completing his education he came back to his realm.[1]

Political organisation.

According to Kauṭilya, the Mallas were a Saṃgha or corporation of which the members called themselves Rājās just as the Licchavis did and the commentator, Buddhaghosa, also calls them Rājās.[2] A passage in the Majjhima Nikāya,[3] in giving an illustration of saṃghas and gaṇas, mentions the Licchavis and the Mallas, showing that the Mallas were a typical example of a saṃgharājya. The accounts given above show that the Mallas of Pāvā and Kuśînārā had their respective Santhāgāras or Mote Halls where all matters both political and religious were discussed. We have seen that a new council-hall called Ubbhaṭaka had been built by the Mallas of Pāvā but was still unused

1. Fausboll, *Dhammapada* (old edition) p. 211.
2. *Dialouges of the Buddha.* pt. III. p. 201
3. *Majjhima Nikāya,* Vol. I. p. 231.

when the Buddha visited their city in the course of his peregrinations, and it was there that they invited him to deliver his discourses to them. We have also seen the Mallas assembled and doing business in their Mote-Hall when Ânanda went to them with the message of the impending death of the Master; and again, the Mallas assembled in the Saṇthāgāra to discuss the procedure to be followed in the disposal of the dead body and afterwards to discuss the claims put forward by the various Kṣatriya kings and peoples.

Manly sports-Wrêstling.

It seems that the Mallas were a martial race and were devoted to such manly sport as wrestling.[1] It is impossible that the word 'Malla' denoting a wrestler by profession was derived from the tribal name of this brave people.

Malla officers.

In the Mahāparinibbāṇa Suttanta as given in the Dīgha Nikāya, there is the mention of a set of officers called Malla Suṇisā and Purisas[2] among the Mallas of Kuśînārā, about whose functions we are quite in the dark. But Professor Rhys Davids takes them to be a class of subordinate servants.[3]

Dr. D. R. Bhāndārkar says that the inde-

1. Jātaka (Cowell's edition), Vol. II. p. 65.
2. Dîgha Nikāya, Vol. II. p. 159.
3. Buddhist India, p. 21.

pendence of the Mallas as an oligarchical republic appears to have been destroyed by the ambitious Magadhan monarch, Ajātaśatru, and their dominions were annexed to the empire that was gradually growing up in Magadha.[1]

Independence crushed—dominions annexed.

The Mallas appear to have been usually on friendly terms with their neighbours, the Licchavis, with whom they had many ties of kinship, though, as was quite inevitable, there were occasional rivalries between the two democratic states as the story of Bandhula shows. One day Bandhula, a Mallian general, drove his chariot to Vaiśālī, the capital of the Licchavis, passed the threshold of Mahāli, a Licchavi, with his wife Mallikā who wanted to go and bathe and drink the waters of the tank where the members of the kings' families used to get water for the ceremonial sprinkling. Mahāli heard the clattering noise (rattling sounds) of the chariot and told the Licchavis of his apprehension of danger. The Licchavis guarded the tank well, spreading an iron net over it. The Mallian general came down from his chariot, put the guards to flight by means of his sword and burst through the iron net-work and in the tank bathed his wife and gave her water to drink ; he then left the place with his wife in the chariot. The guards

Dispute between the two neighbouring confederate clans—the Mallas and the Licchavis.

1. *Carmichael Lectures*, 1918, p. 79.

narrated the event to the Licchavis. The kings of the Licchavis being angry informed Mahāli of it. Mahāli asked them not to go further but to return. Notwithstanding his advice, five hundred kings mounting their chariots set out to capture Bandhula who 'sped a shaft and it cleft the heads of all the chariots and passed right through the five hundred kings.' They being wounded followed him. He stopped his chariot and said, "I cannot fight with the dead." He then asked them to loose the girdle of the first man who fell dead before they could unfasten it. They were asked to go back to their homes and were ordered to instruct their wives and children to make necessary arrangements for their affairs and then drop their armours. They did so and all of them became lifeless.[1]

Philosophy

Philosophy was much discussed by the Mallians. Serious philosophical problems of sati, samādhi, viriya, saddhā, dukkha, etc., did not escape their attention as may be seen from the following incidents: Bhadragakogāmaṇī, an upāsaka, went to the Buddha and enquired of the cause of the arising of suffering and the overcoming of suffering. Buddha replied that he (Bhadragako) did not believe that the enquiry could be answered by exemplifications from past and future occurrences. So Buddha wanted to instruct

1. Dhammapada (Fausboll)., old edition, pp. 218-220.

him about it by means of the present happenings. The Lord said, "Is there anyone in Uruvelakappa who if killed or imprisoned or injured or blamed produces trouble in your mind?" Gāmaṇī replied in the affirmative. The Buddha said, "What is the cause of it? There must be some one here against whom if something be performed, the performance of that act surely produces trouble in your mind." The Lord replied, "The reason of this is that you have attachment towards that one and you have not attachment towards the other. Attachment is not the effect of this life but of the past life." The Buddha cleared his doubts as to his existence in the past. He further said, "There is attachment towards mother for the simple reason that he is born in her womb and for this he is troubled over her disease and death and thereby it is proved that there is a connection between this life and the next. Attachment is the root of our trouble and the uprooting of it is the uprooting of suffering."[1]

Living among the Mallas in Uruvelakappa, he told the Bhikkhus that the four senses (saddhā, viriya, sati and samādhi) can be fully realised by the acquisition of sublime knowledge.[2]

Shortly before the passing away of the

1. *Saṁyutta Nikāya* pt. IV. pp 327-346.
2. Ibid, pt. V. pp. 228-229,

Lord while dwelling in the Śāla-grove of the Mallas at Kuśînārā, he advised the Mallian Bhikkhus, who were present, to bear in mind the following instruction, being ardent and strenuous :— "Vayadhammā Saṃkhārā"[1] (all Saṃkhāras are subject to decay).

Before the advent of Jainism and Buddhism, the Mallas were followers of the Brahmanical faith. One of their shrines called Makuṭa Bandhana, to the east of Kuśînārā, is mentioned in connection with the death of the Buddha where his dead body was carried for cremation. There is, however, no indication of the kind of worship that was performed at this place.

Early Religion-Brahmanical.

Jainism found many followers among the Mallas as among the other races of Northern India. The accounts we get in the Buddhist Literature of the schism that appeared in the Jaina Church after the death of Mahāvīra amply prove this. At Pāvā the followers of Nigaṇṭha Nātaputtạ were divided after the death of their great Tîrthaṅkara. We find that there were both ascetics and lay devotees among these Jainas, for we read that on account of these disputations among the ascetics, "even the lay disciples of the white robe, who followed Nātaputta, showed themselves shocked, repelled and indignant at

Jainism.

1. *Saṁyutta Nikāya* Vol. I. p. 158.

the Nigaṇṭhas."[1] These lay Jainas appear from this passage to have been draped in white robes, just as the śvetambaras are at the present day. The Buddha as well as Sāriputta, one of his principal disciples, seem to have taken advantage of the schism that appears to have overtaken the Jaina church on the death of their founder for propagation of the rival faith. In the Pāsādika Suttanta, we find that it is Cunda, the novice of Pāvā, who brings the news of the death of the great Tîrthaṅkara, Mahāvīra, to Ânanda at Sāmagāma in the Malla country and the latter at once saw the importance of the event and said, "Friend Cunda, this is a worthy subject to bring before the Exalted One. Let's go to him and tell him about it." They hastened to the Buddha who delivered a long discourse.[2]

Buddhism.

Buddhism appears to have attracted many followers among the Mallas, some of whom like the venerable Dabba the Mallian, attained a high and respectable position among the brethren. We read in the Cullavagga,[3] "Now at that time the venerable Dabba the Mallian who had realised Arhatship when he was seven years old, had entered into possession of every

1. *Dialogues of the Buddha* pt. III. p. 203.
2. *Ibid.*, p 112.
3. *Vinaya Texts*, pt. III. p. 4. foll.

(spiritual gift) which can be acquired by a disciple; there was nothing left that he ought still to do, nothing left that he ought to gather up of the fruit of his past labour." On account of his virtues, he was appointed, after due election by the Buddhist Saṃgha, a regulator of lodging places and apportioner of rations. He was so successful in the discharge of these duties which required a great deal of patience and tact that he was considered by the Saṃgha to be possessed of miraculous powers. But there were some, like the followers of Metteya and Bhummajaka, who became envious and set the Bhikkhunī Mettiyā and Vaddha, the Licchavi, to bring about his fall and expulsion from the Saṃgha, but their evil intentions were discovered and the venerable Dabba the Mallian was exculpated from the charges brought against him.

Khaṇḍasumana, reborn in the family of a Malla rājā at Pāvā, entered the order and acquired six-fold Abhiññā.[1]

Once Buddha was in the country of the Mallas named Uruvelakappa. One day he asked Ânanda to stay there and himself left for Mahāvana to spend the day. While Ânanda was staying there, a householder named Tapusso, probably a Mallian, came to him and told him that he was so much absorbed in the enjoyment

1. *Psalms of the Brethren*, p. 90.

of sensual pleasures that he was never averse to wordly life. He (the householder) further told him that even a young man was satisfied with the religion and teachings of the Lord. He asked him as to the cause of it. Ânanda took him to Buddha while he was spending the day at Mahāvana. Ânanda having informed the Buddha, Buddha said that such a state of things happened with him also before attaining enlightenment. He who has not seen and thought of the evil effect of sensual pleasures and he who has not thought of the fruition of emancipation cannot bend his mind towards emancipation. This is the cause of not being able to make oneself averse to wordly life. Buddha said that when he succeeded in seeing and thinking of the evil effect of sensual pleasures and of the fruition of emancipation, he realised the first stage of meditation. When he realised the first stage, the thinking of enjoyment of sensual pleasures became a malady to him; when he realised the second stage, the first stage appeared trifling to him and so on up to the fourth stage. When he realised all the jhānas together with the āyatanas, his mind was bent upon nirvāṇa. Because of his realising the jhānas together with the āyatanas and the nirvāṇa and because of his thwarting the enjoyment of sensual pleasures, he was successful in being foremost, in the

Devabrahmā and the Māra worlds, amongst the Samaṇas and the Brāhmaṇas.[1]

Roga, a Mallian, asked Ânanda whether the Buddha would accept potherbs and meal from his hands. Accordingly, Ânanda asked the Lord whether the presents would be acceptable. The Lord replied in the affirmative. When Roga actually took those presents to him, the Lord asked him to hand them over to the Bhikkhus. He did so and the Bhikkhus were satisfied with them. Roga then sat on one side. When the Blessed One finished his meal, he 'taught, and incited, and conversed, and gladdened' him 'with religious discourse.' At last Roga rose from his seat and departed.[2]

Sīha was reborn in the country of the Mallas in the family of a Rājā. As soon as he saw the Buddha, he saluted him and being attracted, he sat on one side. The Buddha noticing the trend of his thought, taught him the Norm. He entered the Buddhist order and spent his days in the forest but he could not concentrate. Seeing this, the Master advised him to cherish good Norm within himself and to swiftly renounce the 'piled up lease of birth.' This advice of the Lord had a beneficial effect on him and he was able to develop insight and acquire saintship.[3]

---

1. *Aṅguttara Nikāya*, Vol. IV, pp. 438-448.
2. S. B. E., Vol. XVII. p. 139.
3. *Psalms of the Brethren.* p. 80.

The respect and veneration with which the Mallas looked upon the Buddha will appear from how they met him when his last moment was approaching and also from the great liberality and magnificence with which they cremated the corpse and the care and consideration with which they treated the remains.

CHAPTER III.

The Sakyas.

The importance of the Śākyas

The Śākyas have acquired a very great importance in Indian history owing to the Buddha having been born among them. Though a comparatively small clan yet in the rugged fastness of the lower Himalayas, the Śākyas had built up a powerful principality at the time the great teacher was born.

Kapilavastu

General Cunningham and Mr. Carleyle identify the city of Kapilavastu with Bhūila, a village in the Basti district at the foot of the Nepal mountains, about 25 miles north-east from Faizabad, 12 miles north-west from Basti, and 120 miles north of Benares.[1] Its distance from Rājagaha, Vaiśālī and Sāvatthī was sixty yojanas or four hundred and fifty miles, fifty yojanas or three hundred and seventy-five miles and six or seven yojanas or fifty or sixty miles respectively.[2] Dr. Rhys Davids says that the recent discovery of the tope built by the Śākyas over the portion of the relics of the Buddha which fell to their share finally settles that it must have

1. Monier Williams, *Buddhism*, p. 389.
2. Rhys Davids, *Buddhist India*, p. 17. F.

been situated just on the borders of the British and Nepalese territory.[1]

The celebrated Chinese pilgrim, Fā-Hien, who visited India in the fourth century B. C. says that white elephants and lions infested the neighbourhood of Kapilavastu, against which the people had to be on their guard.[2] The country was thinly populated. He noticed towers at Kapilavastu set up in the various places, viz., where prince Siddhārtha left the city by the eastern gate, where his chariot was made to turn back to the palace, where his horoscope was cast by the sage Asita, where the elephant was struck by Nanda and others, where the arrow going 30 li in south-easterly direction penetrated into the earth and produced a fountain of water which quenched the thirst of travellers in later generations, where Suddhodana was met by his son after having acquired supreme wisdom, where 500 Śākya converts honoured Upāli, and where the children of the Śākyas were massacred by King Vidūdabha.[3]

Later on, Hiuen Tsang who visited India in the seventh century A. D. narrates that Kapilavastu, the country of the Śākyas, was about 4,000 li in circuit. The royal precincts built of brick were within the city measuring

1. Ibid., p. 17.
2. *Travels of Fā-Hien and Sang-Yun* by S. Beal, pp. 88-98.
3. *Travels of Fā-Hien* by Beal, pp. 85-87.

14 or 15 li round.[1] He says that long after the passing away of the Buddha, the topes and shrines were built in or near Kapilavastu.[2] The villages were few and desolate. The monasteries (Samghārāmas) which were then in ruins were more than one thousand in number. There still existed a samghārāma near the royal precincts which contained about 3,000 (read 30) followers who read 'the little vehicle of the Sammitiya school.' There were two deva temples where different sectarians worshipped. There were some dilapidated foundation walls, the remains of the proper palace of king Suddhodana, above which, a vihāra (monastery) was built containing a stūpa of the king. Near it, was a foundation in ruins representing the sleeping palace of the Queen Mahāmāyā. Above it, a vihāra was built containing a figure of the Queen. Close by, stood a vihāra where the Bodhisatta entered the womb of his mother. A stūpa was built to the north-east of 'the palace of spiritual conception' of the Bodhisatta.[3] To the north-west of the capital, many stūpas were built where king Viḍūḍabha massacred the Śākyas.[4]

The cultivated land was rich and fertile. The climate of the country was bracing.

---

1. *Beal's Records of the Western World*, Vol. II. pp. 13-14.
2. *Watters'on Yuan Chwang*, Vol. II. p. 4.
3. *Beal's Records of the Western World*, Vol. II., pp. 14-15.
4. Ibid, Vol. II. p. 14.

According to Dr. Rhys Davids, there were villages round the rice-fields and the cattle roamed about in the outlying forest. The jungles which were occasionally resorted to by robbers divided one village from another.[1]

Another Sakya town.

Mention is made of another Śākya town named Khomadussa. It was so called on account of its abundant produce of linen cloth.[2]

People—character.

It is stated in the Jātaka that the Śākyas were a haughty people. They were so very haughty that they did not do obeisance to Siddhārtha on the ground that he was younger in age. But they were afterwards made to do so on seeing a miracle performed by him.[3] Hiuen Tsang saw them obliging in manners.[4] They did not kill any living thing, 'not even a black beetle.'[5] Cattle and rice supplied their only means of livelihood.[6]

Marriage.

The Śākya peasants enjoyed rights in common.[7] There was a law among the Śākyas that no man was permitted to marry more than one wife. But special privilege was given to Suddhodana as he

1. *Buddhist India*, pp. 20-21.
2. *The Book of the Kindred Sayings* pt, I. p. 233.
3. *Jātaka* (Cowell's) Vol. VI. pp. 246-247.
4. Beal's *Records of the Western World*, Vol, II. p, 14.
5. Rockhill., *Life of the Buddha.* p. 117.
6. Rhys Davids., *Buddhist India* , pp 20.
7. Ibid., p. 20.

conquered the hillmen of the Pāṇḍava tribe who were raiding the Śākya country.[1] They had a custom that when a child was born, it was carried to the temple of Iśvara-Deva[2] to be presented to the god.

Education.

There was a technical college of the Śākyas in the mango-grove. The translators on the authority of the Sumaṅgalavilāsinī, the commentary of the Dīgha Nikāya by Buddhaghosa, say, "it was a long terraced mansion made for the learning of crafts."[3] There was also a school of archery at Kapilavastu where the Śākyas were trained.[4]

Origin.

The Śākyas of Kapilavastu claimed to be Kṣatriyas. As soon as they heard of the news of the passing away of the Lord, they demanded a portion of the relics of the Buddha, saying, "Bhagavā amhākaṃ ñātī seṭṭho."[5] (The Blessed one was the chief of our kinsmen.) The Śākyas traced their line back to King Okkāka. King Okkāka desired to have the son of his favourite queen on the throne. Consequently he sent into exile his elder children, Okkāmukha, Karaṇḍa, Hatthinika and

1. Rockhill., *Life of the Buddha*, p. 15.
2. The temple contains a stone image of the god in the posture of rising and saluting. Watters' On Yuan Chwang Vol. II. p. 13.
3. Dialogues of the Buddha, Vol. IV. pt. III. p. III F.
4. Watters' *On Yuan Chwang*, Vol. II., p. 13.
5. *Dīgha Nikāya*, Vol. II, p. 165.

Sinipura, who went to dwell on the slopes of the Himālayas, on the borders of a lake where a big oak (sako) tree stood. They married their sisters to preserve the purity of their blood. The king had a slave girl named Disā. A black baby was born to her. As soon as it was born, it said, "Wash me, mother, bathe me, mother. Let me be rid, mother, of this dirt, so shall I be of use to you."

People said, "This fellow speaks as soon as it is born. It is a black thing (kaṇha) that is born, a devil has been born." The Kaṇhāyaṇas were the descendants of this black baby. It is thus stated in the Ambaṭṭha Suttanta:—"Yes, but if one were to follow up your ancient name and lineage, Ambaṭṭha, on the father's and the mother's side, it would appear that the Śākyas were once your masters, and that you are the offspring of one of their slave girls."[1]

In the Viṣṇupurāṇa we meet with the name of Śākya, a king of the Ikṣāku dynasty. Vrihadvala, a king of the same line, was the father of Vrihatkṣana, whose son Gurukkhepa begot Vatsa who begot Vatsabuha. Vatsabuha begot Prativyoma who begot Divākara. Sahadeva was the son of Divākara and he had a son named Vrihadeva who begot Bhānuratha, who had a son named Supratika. He in turn got a son

1. *Dialogues of the Buddha*, Vol. II., pp. 114-115

Marudeva. Sunakkhatra, Kinnara, Antarikkha, Suvarṇa, Amitrajit, Vrihadrāja and Dharmi were the direct lineal descendants of Marudeva and the ancestors of Kritañjaya who was the great grandfather of Śākya whose father was Sañjaya and whose grandfather was Ranañjaya.[1]

The Tibetan account is that one day King Virudhaka enquired of his courtiers about his beautiful sons. They told the king of his sons' adventures. The king exclaimed, "The daring youngmen, the daring youngmen." And for this marked characteristic they came to be known as Śākyas.[2] Bharata, the commentator of Amarkoṣa, says, "Śāka is a kind of tree. A king of the Ikṣāku dynasty is known as Śākya because he lives near that sāka tree." His posterity was known as Śākyas.

Prince Okkāmukha was the eldest son of Okkāka. His sons and grandsons were Nipuṇa, Candimā, Candamukha, Sivisaṃjaya, the great king Vessantara, Jāli, Sīhavāhana and Sīhassara.

Sakya Kings.

The sons and grandsons of King Sīhassara were 82,000 in number of whom Jaysena was the last.[3] Śākya Añjana's queen was Yasodharā who bore two daughters, Māyā and Prajāpatī, and also two sons. One of the two sons was Śākya Suppa-

1. *Viṣṇu Purāṇa*, pt. IV; Ch. 22.
2. Rockhill., *Life of the Buddha*, p. 12.
3. Geiger's translation of the *Mahāvaṃsa*, p. 11.

buddha whose queen Amitā had two children. Suddhodana's queens were Māyā and Prajāpatī (Pajāpatī). He had a son by his wife Māyā, named Gautama Buddha who was famous as the Śākya lion or the lion amongst the Śākyas (Śākyasiṃha).[1]

The minds of the Śākya royal princes and nobles were so enlightened by the Buddha that they were able to realise "the perfect fruit of righteousness."[2] Nandupananda and Kuṇḍadana, two principal nobles, and other persons of the Śākya clan became recluses.[3] Upāli, son of Atalī, followed their example. Then the other princes and the sons of the chief minister renounced the world.[4] At the request of the Buddha many Śākyas became recluses.[5] They were well provided for.[6] The life of the Śākya recluse was so attractive that Sumaṅgala (reborn in a poor family) became a hermit. They were respected for their simplicity of life.[7] They used to shave their heads, put on yellow robes and carry alms-bowl.[8] Seldom could they find time to sleep as they had too many duties to attend to.[9]

Sakya recluses.

1. Geiger's translation of the *Mahāvaṁsa*, p. 12.
2. S. B. E, Vol. XIX. p. 226. 3. Ibid., pp. 226-227.
4. Ibid., p. 227. 5. Ibid, pp, 226-227.
6. Psalms of the Brethren, p. 81. 7. Ibid, p. 47.
8. Mricchakoṭika, Act. VIII. pp. 125-126. (Jivānanda Vidyāsāgara's edition).
9. Chārudatta, Act III. p. 53

There was a residence at Kapilavastu provided by the community for recluses of all schools.[1]

Mahāpajāpatī Gotamī asked the Buddha to allow her to enter his order but the request was not granted. Whereupon she ordered her hairdresser to cut off her hair, and wearing yellow robes, she took the wives of 500 young Śākya nobles, who had already renounced the world, with her to Vaiśālī where the Master was. Again she asked the permission of the Lord to enter the order and he readily agreed. Her associates were also ordained at the same time.[2]

Mahapajapati Gotami and the Buddha.

At the time of the Buddha Gautama, Tissā was reborn at Kapilavastu among the Śākyas. She renounced the world with Mahāpajāpatī Gotamī and became spiritually so developed that she attained Arhatship.[3]

Tissa and the Buddha.

Vipassī was reborn at Kapilavastu as the daughter of Khemaka, the Śākya. She was called Nandā the Fair for her great beauty and amiability. Her young kinsman and suitor Corabhūta died on the day on which she was to choose him from amongst her suitors. She had to leave the

Vipassi and the Buddha.

1. *Buddhist India*, p. 20.
2. *Psalms of tho Sisters*, p. 7.
3. *Ibid.*, pp. 12-13.

world against her will. Though she entered the order, she could not forget that she was beautiful. Fearing that the Buddha would rebuke her, she used to avoid his presence. The Buddha knew that the time had come for her to acquire knowledge and asked Mahāpajāpatī Gotamī to bring all the Bhikkhunis before him to receive instruction. Nandā sent a proxy for her. The Buddha said, "Let no one come by proxy." So she was compelled to come to him. The Buddha by his supernatural power conjured up a beautiful woman who became transformed into an old and fading figure. It had the desired effect and she became an Arahat.[1]

Theri Mitta.

Mittā, finally reborn in the royal family of the Śākyas at Kapilavastu, left the world with Mahāpajāpatī Gotamī. After the necessary training, she soon attained Arhatship (saintship).[2]

Theri Sundari Nanda and the Buddha.

Sundarī Nandā was reborn in the royal family of the Śākyas. She was known as the beautiful Nandā. Thinking about the fact that her elder brother, her mother, her brother, her sister and her nephew had renounced the world, she left the world. Even after her renunciation, she was obsessed with the idea of her beauty and would not approach the Master lest she should be

1. *Psalms of the Sisters*, pp. 22-23.
2. *Ibid.*, p. 29.

reproached for her folly. The Lord taught her in the same way as he did in the case of Nandā the fair. She listened to the Master's teachings and enjoyed the benefit of the fruition of the first stage of sanctification. He then instructed her saying, "Nandā, there is in this body not even the smallest essence. It is but a heap of bones covered with flesh and smeared with blood under the shadow of decay and death." Afterwards she became an Arhat.[1]

Government.

The administrative and judicial affairs of the Śākya clan were discussed in their Santhāgāra or Mote-Hall at Kapilavastu. A young Brahmin named Ambaṭṭhā who went to Kapilavastu on business had the opportunity of visiting the Mote-Hall of the Śākyas where he saw the young and the old seated on grand seats.[2] That King Pasenadī of Kośala should marry one of the daughters of the Śākya chiefs was decided in it Among the Śākyas, there was only one chief who bore the title of Rājā and was elected by the people. According to Dr. Rhys Davids, he had to preside over the sessions and when no sessions were held, he had to conduct the business of the state. Once Bhaddiya, a young cousin of the Buddha took the title of Rājā and Suddhodana was styled a Rājā, although he was a simple citizen,

1. *Psalms of the Sisters*, pp. 55-57.
2. *Dialogues of the Buddha.*, Vol. II., p. 113.

Suddhodana the Śākiyan.[1] In the opinion of Dr. Rhys Davids, all the important places had such a hall or pavilion covered with a roof but with no walls in which to conduct their business." "The local affairs of the villages were conducted in open assembly consisting of the householders, held in the groves.........which formed so distinctive a feature of each village in the long and level alluvial plain."[2] A contrary view is held by the Chinese travellers, Hiuen Tsang, Fā-hien and Sung-Yun. According to them there was no government at Kapilavastu. There existed a congregation of priests and about ten families of laymen.[3] Each town appointed its own ruler and there was no supreme ruler.[4] In the face of the authorities quoted above we cannot rely on the accounts given by the Chinese pilgrims.

Dr. D. R. Bhāndārkar says that Kula or clan sovereignty was prominent among the Śākyas. Kula, which was more extensive than the family, was the lowest political unit amongst the political Saṃghas. To quote his words, Kula "denotes not simply the domination of a chief over his clan but also and principally his supremacy over the territory occupied by that clan." Śākya

1. *Buddhist India*, p. 19.
2. *Ibid*, p. 20.
3. Beal., *Travels of Fā-hien and Sung-Yun*, pp. 85-87.
4. Beal., *Records of the Western World*, Vol. II, p. 14.

country was governed by one ruler but was not solely occupied by the Śākyas, there were Brahmins, artisans and traders.[1]

A new Mote-Hall of the Śākyas was raised at Kapilavastu when the Buddha was dwelling at the Nigrodhārāma in the Mahāvana which was close to it. At their request the Buddha inaugurated the hall and a series of ethical discourses lasting the whole of the night were delivered by him and Ânanda and Moggallāna.[2]

The Sakyas and Kosala.

Once Pasenadī, King of Kośala, carried away by his horse reached Kapilavastu alone, and roaming about hither and thither came to the garden of Mahānāman. Here he saw the beautiful Mallikā who was well versed in the sāstras and asked her as to whose garden it was and was told that it belonged to Śākya Mahānāman. He then got down and wanted some water to wash his feet with. She brought it. Again she was asked to bring some water with which to wash his face and she brought it and the king washed his face with it. Afterwards he wanted some water to drink which was brought for him in a leaf-cup. Then she was requested by the king to rub his feet which she willingly did. Hardly had she touched his feet when he fell asleep. She thought that the king might

1. *Carmichael Lectures* 1918, pp. 162-164.
2. *Buddhist India.*, p. 20.

have enemies and she closed the gate when the cries of 'open' were heard by her from a multitude of people who wanted to rush in. She did not open the gate. The king awoke and asked her what the matter was. She told him what she did. Her shrewdness and wisdom were admired by the king. Coming to know that she was a slave girl of Mahānāman, he went to her master and expressed his desire to marry her. The master agreed and the king took her with him in great pomp to Srāvastī. But the king's mother was highly displeased as her son had married a slave girl. When Mallikā went to pay respects to her and touched her feet, she at once fell asleep. When she awoke, she thought that such a touch could not but be of a maiden of noble birth, worthy of the family of Kośala. At that time Pasenadī had a wife named Varṣikā famous for her beauty, besides Mallikā well known for her wonderful touch. Shortly afterwards, a son was born to Mallikā who was called Virudhaka or the high-born.[1]

Pasenadī wished to establish connections with the Buddha's family by marriage and wanted to marry one of the daughters of the Śākya chiefs. The Śākyas afterwards decided that it was beneath their dignity to marry one

1. Rockhill's *Life of the Buddha*, pp. 75-77.

of the daughters to the king of Kośala.[1] A girl named Vāsabha Khattiyā, a daughter by a slave girl of one of their leading chiefs, was sent by the Śākyas to the king.

The Śākyas became the vassals of King Pasenadī of Kośala who received homage from them and they treated him in the same way as the king treated the Buddha.[2]

King Pasenadī had great admiration for the Buddha who was a Śākya. The king went to him and rubbed his feet out of devotion to him. He admitted that he never found a teacher like him. He further said, "Worldly life is full of civil strifes as people have not yet realised the Dharma of the Tathāgata.[3]

Viḍūḍabha when he came of age, found out that the Śākyas had deceived his father Pasenadī by giving him a daughter of a slave girl to marry. He resolved to take revenge upon them. After ascending the throne, he invaded the Śākya country, took their city and slew many of them without any distinction of age or sex.

Having annihilated the Śākyas, five hundred Śākya girls were taken by him for his harem to celebrate his victory. The girls who were full of rage and hatred said that they would never submit to the king. They abused him

---

1. Dr. Rhys Davids., *Buddhist India.*, p. II.
2. *Dialogues of the Buddha*, pt. III. p 80.
3. *Majjhima Nikāya*, Vol. II, pt. I, pp. 118-124.

and his family. On hearing this, the king was enraged and gave orders to kill them. The officers, according to the orders of the king, cut off their hands and feet and threw them into a ditch. The girls sought the aid of the Buddha who saw their disrtess and ordered a Bhikkhu to go to them and to preach before them the most profound doctrine of the Buddha. They having heard the instructions of the Buddha, attained "the purity of the eyes of law." They then died and were all reborn in heaven.[1]

There is a different version of the above account stated in the Viḍūḍakāvadānam of the Avadānakalpalatā.[2] According to it, Viḍuḍaka slaughtered 77,000 Śākyas and stole 1,000 boys and girls. One day when he was eulogising his own prowess in his court, the stolen Śākya girls said, "Why is this pride when death is inevitable to a man bound by action?" The king heard this and became angry and ordered his men to cut off the hands of the girls.

Dr. Rhys Davids says that the motives which led Viḍuḍaka to attack and conquer the Śākyas were most probably similar to the political motives which afterwards persuaded Ajātaśatru

1. Beal's *Records of the Western World*, Vol. II. pp. 11-12.
2. 11th Pallava, Avadānakalpalatā (Bibliotheca Indica series).

to attack and conquer the Licchavis of Vaiśālī.[1] We think that the only reason of Viḍūḍabha invading the Śākya country and massacring a large number of the Śākyas was that they, when asked by his father, King Pasenadī, to marry a Śākya girl, deceived him (Pasenadī) by sending Vāsavakhattiyā, a girl of low birth.

It is stated in the Mahāvaṃsa Ṭīkā that during the life-time of the Buddha, some Śākyas being oppressed by Vidūdabha fled to the Himalayas where they built a beautiful city which was known as the Moriyanagara (Mauryanagara) on account of the spot always resounding with the cries of peacocks.[2] The Buddhists hold that Aśoka and the Buddha were of the same family as the former descended from Candragupta who was a son of the Queen of one of the kings of Moriyanagara.[3]

1. *Buddhist India*, pp. 11-12.
2. *Mahāvaṁsa Ṭīkā* (Ceylonese edition) pp. 119-121.
3. Beal's *Records of the Western World*, Vol. I. Intro p. XVII.

CHAPTER IV.

Minor Clans.

Besides the clans of which some account has been given in the previous chapters, there are a few others occasionally referred to in the Buddhist texts, particularly in the Book of the Great Decease. They may be enumerated as follows :—

Enumeration.

1. The Bulis of Allakappa.
2. The Koliyas of Rāmagāma.
3. The Moriyas of Pipphalivana.
4. The Bhaggas of Suṃsumāra Hill.
5. The Kālāmas of Kesaputta.

"There are," as Dr. Rhys Davids points out, "several other names of tribes of which it is not yet known whether they were clans or under monarchical government. We have only one instance of any tribe, once under a monarchy, reverting to the independent state. And whenever the supreme power in a clan became hereditary, the result seems always to have been an absolute monarchy, without legal limitations of any kind."[1]

Enumeration not Complete

The five clans or tribes mentioned above are mere passing shadows in early Buddhist

1. *Buddhist India*, p. 23.

records, there being hardly any data for an historical account of them. The Book of the Great Decease[1] mentions the Bulis of Allakappa, the Koliyas of Rāmagāma and the Moriyas of Pippalivana, along with the Licchavis of Vesālī, the Śākyas of Kapilavatthu and others, as so many distinct Kṣatriya clans or corporations, claiming shares of the bodily remains of the Buddha Gautama on the ground that like the deceased master they were all of the Kṣatriya tribe. The message sent by each of these clans to the Mallas of Kuśīnārā is as follows: "The Blessed One belonged to the soldier caste, we too are of the soldier caste. We are worthy to receive a portion of the relics of the Blessed One. Over the remains of the Blessed one will we put up a sacred cairn and in their honour will we celebrate a feast."[2] The claimants are said to have obtained their respective shares of relics, which they enshrined with customary ceremonies. The Bulis of Allakappa and the Koliyas of Rāmagāma had the good fortune to obtain one share each of the bodily remains while the Moriyas of Pipphalivana had to be satisfied with a share of the ashes as they were rather late in sending their

Origin.

Distribution of the Buddha's relics.

The Bulis and the Koliyas.

1. *Dīgha Nikāya*, II. p. 164. foll.
2. *Buddhist Suttas*, S. B. E. Vol. XI. p. 132.

messenger to Kusīnārā. The existing Buddhist traditions all agree in bearing out the fact of redistribution of the relics of the Buddha in the time of King Aśoka with the exception of those enshrined at Rāmagāma by the Koliyas. The legend from the Aśokāvadāna which has been summarised by late Dr. Vincent Smith is as follows :—"The Avadāna story is that when King Aśoka desired to distribute the sacred relics of the body of Buddha among the eighty-four thousand stūpas erected by himself, he opened the stūpa of the Urn, wherein King Ajātaśatru had enshrined the cremation relics collected from seven of the eight original stūpas. The eighth, that at Rāmagāma, was defended by the guardian Nāgas, who would not allow it to be opened. The relics thus withdrawn from the stūpa of the Urn were distributed among eighty-four thousand stūpas, 'resplendent as the autumn clouds,' which were erected in a single day by the descendant of the Mauryas."[1] A similar legend can be gathered from the Sinhalese Chronicles and other later Pāli works, particularly Buddhaghosa's commentary[2] on the Mahāparinibbāṇa Suttanta. The evidence of the Pāli Canonical texts themselves amply corroborates the truth of the later legends barring certain

The Moriyas.

1. Vincent Smith—*Aśoka*, 2nd edition, pp. 225-226.
2. *Sumaṅgala-Vilāsinī*, Burmese edition, pt. II p. 183. foll.

Cremation of the Buddha's body and disposal of the relics.

details which have a special importance of their own. The epilogues attached to the *Book of the Great Decease* and the *Buddhavaṁsa* prove that the sacred relics of Buddha's body were, after their redistribution, enshrined over the whole of nothern India from Gāndhāra to Kalinga.[1]

The Bhaggas

The Bhaggas of the Suṃsumāra Hill have been casually referred to in some suttas of the Majjhima and the Samyutta Nikāyas,[2] but it is difficult to say from these references who they were and what social and political relations they had with the other clans of Nothern India. There can be no doubt about the fact that the Suṃsumāra Hill was used as a fort. The hill was situated in a deer park at Bhesakalāvana. In the lifetime of the Buddha lived Prince Bodhi, the heir-apparent to the then reigning king of the Bhaggas, who became one of the followers of the Buddha.[3] When the Buddha was amongst them, the householder, Nakulapitā, went to him and spoke to him thus, "I have become old and wearied, let the Lord admonish me and instruct me for my eternal happiness." He

1. Dīgha Nikāya II. p. 167. The Buddhavaṁsa and the Cariyā Piṭaka, p. 68. I. J. P. T. S. 1882. Edited by the Rev. Richard Morris.
2. *Majjima Nikāya*. Vol. I. pp. 332-338 ; Vol. II. pt. 1. pp. 91-97 *Saṁyutta Nikāya* pt. IV. p. 116. pt. III. pp. 1-5.
3. *Bodhirājakumāra Sutta, Majjhima Nikāya.*

afterwards became one of the devotees of the Master at Bhesakalāvana.[1]

The Kalamas

As regards the Kālāmas of Kesaputta, our information is very meagre. There is but a bare mention of them in the Nikāyas. No doubt they existed at the time of the Buddha as a distinct tribe or people. Probably their home or seat of government was in a mountain fastness, not far from the lower Gangetic valley. We are quite in the dark about their origin and other particulars. We must bear in mind that in ancient India the tribe lent its name to the place of its settlement, that is to say, the tribal name became local. The word Kesaputta should be taken in its plural form, denoting the land of the Kesaputtas. The etymology of the name indicates that the tribe traced its descent from a Kesin or a person wearing long locks of hair, i. e. a hermit or Jaṭila. All this is but conjecture. In the Mahāparinibbāṇa Suttanta[2] and other Buddhist texts, ancient and modern, we are introduced to a renowned religious teacher named Âlāra Kālāma, (Sanskrit, Arāḍa Kālāma). One caravan merchant named Pukkusa, a young Mallian, was a disciple of Âlāra Kālāma. Much emphasis was laid by Pukkusa on the spiritual attainments of Kālāma. He said that his preceptor's ecstatic

1. *Saṁyutta Nikāya*, pt. III. pp. 1-5.
2. *Dîgha Nikāya*, Vol. II. pp. 130-131.

trance was so very deep and profound that a long train of heavily laden carts passed by him but he did not perceive them.[1] Âlāra Kālāma might be a Haṭayogin. Buddhaghoṡa says that Âlāra Kālāma was called Âlāra because he was a Dīgha-piṅgala or a hermit of long standing, Kālāma being his family name.[2] It would seem clear that Âlāra Kālāma came of the Kālāma tribe or that he was in some way connected with it. The Buddhist texts represent the Kālāmas as worshippers of the Buddha Gautama who was, before his enlightenment, a disciple of Kālāma, a renowned teacher of philosophy.[3]

The Koliyas.

The name, the Koliyas of Rāmagāma, indicates that the tribe came originally from the same ethnic group as the Koliyas of Devadaha. According to Cunningham, Rāmagāma (Rāmagrāma) is identical with Deokali.[4] There are no historical data for ascertaining the political relations of the Koliyas of Rāmagāma (Rāmagrāma) with the Śākya confederacy. It is stated in the Mahāparinibbāṇa Suttanta of the Dīgha Nikāya that the inhabitants of Rāmagāma belonged to the serpent race.[5]

---

1. *Buddhist Suttas*, S. B. E. Vol. XI, p. 76.
2. *Ibid*, p. 75. f.
3. Kern, *Manual of Indian Buddh sm*, p. 18.
4. Cunningham, *Ancient Geography of India*. p. 423.
5. *Dīgha-Nikāya*. Vol. II, pp. 167.

The Mahāvaṃsa commentary[1] furnishes us with some interesting information about the origin of the Moriyas of Pipphalivana and their connection with the Maurya rulers of Magadha. We are told that there are two theories about the derivation of the name Moriya. According to one theory, the name is derived from 'modiya' meaning pleasing or delightful. The Moriyas were a people who lived in a delightful land. According to the other, the name is connected with 'mora,' peacock. The people came to be known as Moriyas from the fact that the place, where they founded their city, always resounded with the cries of peacocks. It is said that some of the Śākya princes, being hard pressed by Prince Viḍūḍabha, the ambitious and cruel usurper of the throne of Kośala, fled to the Himalayan region where they built a new city round a lake in the forest tract abounding in pepul trees.

The Moriyas.

The above legend about the origin of the Moriyas of Pipphalivana cannot be accepted as an historical fact. When the Moriyas are introduced to us in *the Book of the Great Decease*, they are contemporaries and powerful rivals of the Śākyas of Kapilavatthu or Kapilavastu. Moreover, Viḍūḍabha's invasion of Kapilavatthu and the carnage committed

1. *Mahāvaṁsa-Ṭīkā* (Ceylonese edition) p. 119, foll.

upon its citizens took place, if the tradition is at all to be believed, shortly before the demise of the Buddha. There may be some truth in the implied suggestion that the Moriyas were in some way connected with the Śākyas of Kapilavatthu. With the advance of ethnological researches, it may be found that the matrimonial alliances of the Śākyas with the neighbouring hill peoples brought some new tribes into existence. Further, the Mahāvaṃsa commentary traces the origin of the Maurya rulers of Magadha to the Moriyas of Pipphalivana. Candagutta, the founder of the Maurya dynasty, was born of the chief queen of the Moriyan king of Pipphalivana. This account conflicts with the evidence of Viśākhadatta's Mudrārākṣasa where Candragupta is represented as a Vṛṣala,[1] a person of low birth, an illegitimate son of the last Nanda king by a sūdra woman named Murā. How far Viśākhadatta's account represents the true state of things is a controversial point. But there are many instances where much misconception of history resulted from a conjectural etymology of personal and dynastic names. It appears that the royal family of the Nandas was connected by matrimonial alliance with the Moriyas of Pipphalivana, and this may derive some support from the fact that in earlier and later times, the rulers of Magadha

1. Act. III. pp. 134—136, 141—143, etc.

found it necessary to establish friendly relations, through marriage, with the neighbouring clans, e. g., the Licchavis of Vaiśālī and the Videhans of Mithilā.

It seems certain that the minor clans had much in common with those dealt with in the previous chapters. Their social customs, religious beliefs, laws and administrative systems were substantially the same. It is left to the future historian of India to decide how far the clans under review were instrumental in the colonisation of Bengal, Behar and Assam.

INDEX

INDEX.

Licchavi-dauhitra 7
Licchavigaṇa 72, 73
Licchivi 2 foll.

ERRATA.

Page		Read		instead of	
Page	22	Read	*Ingenious*	instead of	Ingenuous
,,	23	,,	*Līnā*	,,	Līna
,,	24	,,	*And*	,,	and
,,	25	,,	*Explicitly*	,,	Explicity
,,	45	,,	*For*	,,	To
,,	46	,,	*Magnificence*	,,	Magnificience
,,	60	,,	*Loosely*	,,	losely
,,	61	,,	*Magnificent*	,,	Magnificient
,,	62	,,	*Account*	,,	Accouut
,,	86	,,	*when*	,,	that
,,	101	,,	*Taught*	,,	Taugh
,,	101	,,	*Nigaṇṭhaputta*	,,	Nigṇṭhaputta
,,	196	,,	*Distress*	,,	Disrtess
,,	197	,,	*queen*	,,	Queen
,,	201	,,	*Northern*	,,	Nothern

PRINTED BY
Benode Behari Pal, M. Sc.
Bengal Printing Works : Calcutta.